Due to an accident I suffered in September of 2008, I had to have a leg amputated, fight a long recovery from five emergency room surgeries, and deal with the discovery of inoperable cancer around my liver and in my abdomen. Needless to say, the toughness I gained from my days competing as an athlete and teaching and coaching on the collegiate level for over forty years really helped me to persevere in the battle to come back from these setbacks.

*Your Kid's Too Soft* can help you in developing the toughness necessary for your child to overcome the obstacles in athletics and life that only serve to make us stronger and better as people if we will only fight our hardest. I coached Tim's son Steve in our basketball program at Northern State University, so I know firsthand that his theories have worked exceptionally well for one of his own. This is a great book by a great teacher and coach that will lead to greatness for those who use the principles of parenting inside these covers. There is no ride like that of watching your children compete academically and athletically, so enjoy it!

—Don Meyer,
Men's college basketball all-time wins leader and the recipient of the Jimmy V. Perseverance Award at the 2009 ESPN ESPYS.

# your
# kid's
## too
# soft

# your kid's too soft

## welcome to the old school

## tim smiley

TATE PUBLISHING & *Enterprises*

Published by Tate Publishing & Enterprises, LLC
127 E. Trade Center Terrace | Mustang, Oklahoma 73064 USA
1.888.361.9473 | www.tatepublishing.com

Tate Publishing is committed to excellence in the publishing industry. The company reflects the philosophy established by the founders, based on Psalm 68:11,
*"The Lord gave the word and great was the company of those who published it."*

Book design copyright © 2010 by Tate Publishing, LLC. All rights reserved.
*Cover design by Brandon Wood*
*Interior design by Nathan Harmony*

Published in the United States of America

ISBN: 978-1-61663-429-2
1. Education: Parent Participation
2. Education: Students & Student Life
10.06.01

# Dedication

This work is dedicated to my grandkids. Currently that means Madden and Avery Smiley, but will hopefully include more. Hey, sons, Matt and Steve, please work hard at helping your kids to be strong and resilient in this difficult world. I'm sure you will do what every parent should—be the best parents possible.

# Acknowledgments

Four years have been spent trying to identify and partially solve this problem. So many people have helped me that it would be impossible to list them all here. Specific contributions came from a number of my current and recent colleagues at Pomona High School. They would include Dr. Tom Bindel, Suzie Jekel, and Jeff Donnel. The remainder of our current staff (Dan Kerchner, Laura Zarlengo, Scott Pinegar, Chad Barworth, Matt Hulstrom, Jay Jarrell, Nick Dewey, and Dave Wuchner) have kept me both inspired and in-line for the past four years. I could go back thirty-four years worth of science department colleagues, and they would have been as inspirational as all of these guys. Thanks, Dr. Shoemaker, for hiring me. I have been truly blessed. I also need to acknowledge the seven different principals I worked for over thirty-four years. Six of them were great.

On the parental front, I need to thank Dee Hodapp (and her family), along with the family of Tom Keck, for their willingness to share their trials and successes with the raising of their kids. As mentioned earlier, they really are models for how to do it.

I've stolen pearls of wisdom from some famous sources, like Lou Holtz (in a Denver television interview), *ESPN the Magazine* (for the article on Tebucky Jones), and some statistics from the U.S. Census Bureau. Thanks to them for doing their jobs so well.

The Business Department at Black Hills State University and Dean of Business, Dr. Priscilla Romkema, aided me in the design of my survey. Thank you for your time.

Hal Kuczwara shared his college freshmen counseling experiences with me in detail. Thank you, Hal.

One of my former students, Julie Connelly Schlosser, was kind to use her expertise to edit my mistakes. Thanks, Jules.

Finally I need to simultaneously thank my family and my students for thirty-four years. It goes back to when I was the child, and my parents had their job to do with me. All of these experiences have truly been glaring examples of positive interaction and also great blessings for me. I hope everyone else feels the same. Thanks to all one last time.

# Table of Contents

# Introduction

My name is Tim Smiley, and I am an everyday educational soldier who teaches high school kids in America. The year is somewhere between 2004 and 2008, and I am here to tell you about how your child may be doing in our educational system. I have seen a lot of changes in public education, and to be honest, a lot of them are good.

Others, however, seem to be barking up the wrong tree. When a student doesn't do well, everyone begins to look for reasons why. Fair enough. Everyone and everything should be fair game, if one assumes that the real goal is to improve how your kid is doing. This book is for the parent because you need to have a resource that tells you the truth about the state of raising kids and making them productive and responsible.

I will tell you the truth, at least as I see it. We are in the midst of an educational attitude since 2000 with a program called No Child Left Behind. It assumes that every child can learn, will learn, and become a productive American someday. I'm here to tell you that it isn't going to happen. *Every* child will succeed? Additionally, I am betting that what you really care about is how *your* kids will do in the jungle of life they will enter in only a few years. I am not talking about raising your child's standardized test scores. Some people think those things matter the most. I think those scores are a great example of barking up the wrong tree. This will be a pointed approach that will not gloss over issues that are difficult in the real world of parenting.

I am also guessing you love your kid. That really complicates the issue of raising kids, because it can cloud your judgment in about a million ways. This book is written to help you help your son or daughter during those critical years they call high school. Finally, I want your kid to succeed almost as much as you do.

I am a high school science teacher in a Denver area suburban high school, and I have been doing this job for thirty-three years. I have been at Pomona High School for thirty-two years, and I have thoroughly enjoyed my job nearly every day. I would characterize Pomona kids as middle-class, solid, and hardworking. Historically they have operated in a system where they earn what they get in the realm of grades. We have had very few negative issues ever with our students, and I believe that I could teach here for an unlimited amount of time. No, I am not burned out, and I make it a point to laugh every day. It has been so rewarding that it's hard to consider this "work."

So why would I write a book? For years now, I have remarked on how consistent my students have been in their social and educational makeup. More than one teacher has left Pomona for another high school and then commented, "I wish I still had Pomona kids to teach."

Recently, however, there are signs of a quiet sickness brooding among our population. Kids are waning in their academic effort levels. Even though they are still really great kids, something has changed that is making them more hesitant to "bust their tails" on a daily basis. It's been a gradual but definite change, and I think it is symptomatic of typical American students everywhere.

It is also true that high school graduation rates are dropping nationally. I was in the midst of completing year twenty-nine in the spring of 2004, when a specific incident occurred with one of my students (the incident is detailed later in the text). I commented to my first period class on that fateful day in April, "That's it. I'm writing a book."

Am I really qualified to write it? Absolutely. Like my colleagues, I am a daily soldier. I live in the trenches. I have also raised two sons that are in their mid and late twenties. They were Pomona students, and both are eminently successful today. I have concluded, and will convince you it's true, that parents should wake up to how they are raising their kids on a daily basis. I do not believe that ethnicity, economics, or educational backgrounds of the family factor into understanding and solving the problems outlined in this book. What does factor in is the willingness of parents to step up and do the right thing for their kids for as long as they are raising them.

This is a very optimistic book. You would be hard-pressed to find a more optimistic guy than myself when dealing with today's high school kids. I have no intention of retiring in the foreseeable future because I am doing what I want to do every day. Get ready to see the problem, and more importantly, get ready to solve it. For your kid to be a strong and successful adult, you, the parent, need to be that way right now.

# "Sup"

I am a high school science teacher and proud of it. I've taught a number of different science classes to a whole bunch of kids (I'm probably approaching 4,000 students grades nine through twelve in thirty-three years). I've also taught college prep courses like Chemistry and Physics. One of my current classes (Field Geology) is part of our most advanced set of classes called Science Seminar. This class receives college credit from the University of Colorado system.

One of the most unique classes and populations I've ever taught was found in a class called Unified Science. Initially, in the 1980s it was designed for students that struggled with the graduation requirement of a second year of science (currently, there are movements to add a required third year). Mostly, the kids were not highly motivated, and attendance on a daily basis was a major problem. This specific problem has grown to greater magnitude in 2008. That is a wide spectrum of kids, and all of them present unique challenges.

My daily experiences have given me a unique opportunity to observe some interesting patterns in how kids have changed over the years. Are they really much different from the middle-class suburban kids of the midseventies, mideighties, or midnineties? I would say not much. However three things have really changed over the last thirty years.

1.  Hairstyles of both male and female students over time.

2.  The type of music that today's students listen to.

3.  The specific linguistics that they use to address one another as they walk down the halls on a daily basis.

## Has the Music Really Changed That Much?

Many of today's parents of high school kids were students in the heart of the 1980s. Some of you date back to the seventies. I guess the average kid (whoever you were) liked traditional rock and roll in 1975. Groups in favor might have included: The Rolling Stones, Led Zeppelin, The Eagles, etc. Motown was still big. The late seventies brought evolution in musical tastes for some, and the great debate between rock and disco was born.

The eighties saw punk rock explode for some, and the advent of MTV made the changes accelerate. It's hard to believe your favorite band (Van Halen, the Cure, U2, etc.) was taking care of business when you were a high school legend. You all know the rest of the sequence with the eventual arrival of rap or the hip-hop age. I thought it was a fad. I was wrong. It is a phenomenon that has permeated the interest of huge numbers of high school kids, and it crosses every line of economic background, race, gender, etc. I wonder if you, the kids of the 70s and 80s, would say that music has indeed evolved?

## How About the Hall Language?

Let us go to point number three above. I talk about this all the time in my classes. I tell my students that back in the day, we used to walk down the hall, see a buddy approaching, and use this really cool thing called a full sentence. I might have said, "Hey, how's it going today?" Should we still talk in full sentences today? Today's teens seem to be getting away from the practice. Allow me to elaborate.

### A Recent History of Hallway Greetings:

Teachers began to hear differences in the halls by the late 80s, and it currently has accelerated in its demise. Here's the approximate timeline:

1.  About 1989—Thoughts and phrases both go shorter with: "What's up?"

    I heard this solidly for about five years. It didn't seem like a trend at the time

2.  About 1994 or 1995—The *s* goes south, and kids start to say: "What up?"

Now this is a huge savings. Less energy is clearly expended. It sounds a bit more hip, and it won over the entire country. My own sons gave me a steady diet of it.

3. Maybe 1999 or 2000—There is another economy of movement to our current hallway lingo: "Sup."

Are you kidding? Now we are truly de-evolving. You know we are headed down the drain in terms of our verbal skills. All of my students know where this is headed.

*We are destined to become a flock of snake people within the next twenty years.*

Our new and perhaps final response to oncoming friends will be simply a head nod and "Sssss."

Parents, you know this is true. I could not be making this up. And best of all, you see it on a daily basis in your family's lives. You have even allowed your own language skills to change in dealing with your offspring.

While this has to rank as one of the great social discoveries of all time, the question is: "Does it matter?" Maybe it does, and then again, maybe it doesn't. So let me give you a few other changes that have fallen on our student populations over the last thirty years, and we can discuss whether it mattered or not in the sum of their lives.

## Velcro Shoes, Calculators, Etc.

Velcro shoes, calculators, the ability to type and also write well (the new SAT demands it), timeliness to class, moms and dads covering for kids—all need to be analyzed. Their histories give us clues as to what is really important in raising a kid.

## 1. Ability to read a clock or watch

Is this a real question? Yes, it is. Since the advent of digital watches and clocks in the 80s, the potential for kids to struggle with analog clocks has been there. One of my Chemistry students in the early nineties came into class one day with this story. She had been babysitting a seven-year-old child the night before, and she had been told to have him in bed by 9:00 p.m. My student noticed that the time on the clock had reached 8:55 p.m., and so she said to the young guy, "Why don't you go get your pajamas on because it's almost time to go to bed?" His response was something like, "It's not even close to bedtime because it's still only 8:55."

Old school clocks seem to be hanging on, and kids *still* appear to be able to deal with them. Not a big deal.

## 2. Ability to tie one's own shoes

This is a personal experience I saw with my oldest son, Matt. He was preparing to go to kindergarten in 1983, and Matt had to learn how to tie his own shoes before his first day. It was an excruciating process, but like all kids, he finally got it. After a few months, he needed a new pair of shoes, and we went for the big time: Velcro kangaroo shoes with side zips.

While he was the fashion rage in kindergarten for the next two months, he also lost his ability to tie his shoes when the next pair of shoes was purchased. I had to revisit the whole process with him and found direct evidence that *skills must be continually practiced, or they will be lost forever.* Velcro shoes never became big because they can't hold shoes on tightly enough. I was sure they would make it to the NBA on guys like Michael Jordan. It just did not happen. Once again, this was no big deal. Bigger hurdles, however, did loom.

### 3. Ability to do math without a calculator.

Now this seems to be in a different arena of importance. Handheld calculators first appeared in the early to mid-seventies and were really expensive. I had an opportunity to buy one in 1972 or 1973 as a college student, but the minimum cost of the HP scientific calculator was about $250. You may remember (or not) the first programmable calculators had small little program cards to insert in the calculator, and the unit ran a cool $800. Today's versions, mostly made by Texas Instruments, compare at about $15 and $100 respectively and are infinitely more powerful than those of thirty years ago. While this all seems good, some significant problems have emerged with students' ability to understand "sup" with math problems.

The year is 1987, and one of my Chemistry students by the name of Jill has asked me to take part in judging a competition one day after school. It involves ranking the contestants in four categories on a scale of one to ten and then adding up their scores. An example of this would be student X had scores of 3, 8, 9, and 7 in her categories. Of course the total sum of those scores is _____?

You are *not* reaching for a calculator, are you? Jill was. She was also sitting right next to me and noticed that I was watching her use the calculator. She immediately made the excuse that she did not really need it but she only found it to be quicker. I said, "Okay." A few minutes passed, and I said, "So, why are you really using the calculator?" I will never forget her response. Jill said, "Mr. Smiley, I never learned my multiplication tables." I quickly responded, "Nine times seven." Her final response was, "I don't have a clue."

Now here is a case where the injection of "better technology" has actually hurt learning. You may think Jill was a below-average student in the high school setting, but actually she was an A/B student in Chemistry and finished her high school career with a 3.7 GPA. Basically, she was a conscientious student that had to fake some of her basic math skills with the use of the calculator. This experience made me determined to continually try to help kids see the value of understanding basic principles before going more high-tech routes.

Please understand, I am not advocating eliminating technology in the classroom! Here is the most important thing about using the machines of "intelligence": *Students should understand the basic principles involved before they get to touch the shortcut machine.* What would happen if elementary schools banned the use of the calculator for the first six years of education? I believe the math principles would be better learned.

We have all heard the claims that our American kids

are slipping in the arena of math skills compared to their international competition. On average, kids do not feel confident when working with numbers. I would even say today's students fear math. *Steps have to be taken to help them develop that confidence.* Like it or not, math skills can make the difference when determining a kid's future.

## 4. Ability to type

I think it's a crime if kids graduate from high school without the ability to type on a computer. We're in an age when communication skills include many forms of digital communication like e-mail, blogging, etc. The keyboard is a huge communication device in every walk of life and work. Parents, can your son or daughter operate efficiently in a typing or keyboarding mode? Imagine not being able to type in today's setting.

## 5. Ability to be reliable and timely when the occasion calls for it

There is not a more important job quality in the working world than being able to be somewhere on time. Today's students have slipped in this arena, and all of us (educators and parents alike) must band together to help them value this like they should. Sleep can wait, and so can Starbucks.

My colleagues and I seem to discuss on a daily basis the evils of parents calling in to excuse some type of bogus absence for their son or daughter. Students will fall into any habit that they are allowed to. If sleeping in and late arrival is not a problem for the parent, it sure will not be a problem for the kid.

## 6. Willingness to take on the difficult challenge and make their best effort

What really separates students from being average and then vaults them to a higher status? The truth is, most kids are born with a certain adequate level of intellectual ability. Sure, some have excessive intellects, and some fall a bit short. If your son or daughter develops the ability to care about his or her education and a quality work ethic to go with it, they can achieve dizzying heights of success. Parents must help the kids learn to value effort level in their daily lives.

These six areas are only a sampling of the things kids need to develop as they mature into adulthood. I want you, the parents, to see these discussions as opportunities to help your kids develop strengths in their lives. *Remember, strength is always a product of hard work.*

# The Toughest Kid
# in Any Town?

This book is all about helping today's kids become stronger, more independent, and, for lack of a better term, *tougher*. We all have some kind of image about what that means, and it is a highly variable image at that. I am not talking about toughness in any physical or fighting sense, but I rather refer to the term in a mental and emotional way. If parents can raise their son or daughter to be mentally resilient, disciplined, etc., then we all win. These are difficult times. Our society needs more strength, not more softness in our young folks.

That brings us squarely to Mr. Daniel Lazzatti of Orlando, Florida. What are the chances that anyone watching the evening news can randomly find the toughest kid in

America? It may well be that I did exactly that on the evening of May 25, 2007 while watching the *CBS Evening News with Katie Couric*. Actually, I only saw the last two-thirds of the story. I was walking out the door to have dinner with my ex-wife, Claudia Smiley, when she spied the final story of the evening on the incredible kid from Orlando.

Claudia said, "You better watch this. This is exactly what your book is about." I waited for the commercial to end and then sat dumbfounded as Steve Hartman told the story of Daniel Lazzatti in that week's "Assignment America" story.

It was a story of a young man who spent the final two years of his high school career working diligently to achieve a 3.7 GPA. *That's great*, I thought, *but is that special to the point of being national news?* Actually, he had more than a few obstacles in his way, the largest of which was the fact that he was homeless for those two years and lived in a neighbor's backyard tool shed. That's right—living with rakes and shovels. The story was made more incredible by the fact that Daniel had chosen to do this himself and operated without a lot of food and very few luxuries that most would take for granted. His mode of transportation was a small bike he had found in a Dumpster, and he rode it everywhere, even though it didn't have any brakes. He was on a mission to finish his education on a high note. I was pretty amazed.

In the next few days, I researched his high school on the Internet and found his two main counselors. I told them about this book and asked if they thought Daniel would be interested in talking to me if I came to Orlando. He ended up being very excited about how his story fit in my book,

and we set an interview for June 30, 2007. I learned a car-
load about Daniel Lazzatti and about how atypical he was
among American youth. I had found the icon for resiliency.

Cheryl Romaine and Jennifer Eubanks work at
Edgewater High School in the area of exceptional services. The old term for that kind of department was the
special education department, and they indeed both do
some special things for the students of EHS. It turns out
that they began to counsel Daniel during his ninth grade
year because he came to the high school identified as an
exceptional services type of student. Daniel *chose* to leave
that department as he began to understand his educational needs better.

Cheryl and Jen became two of the greatest influences in
making Daniel Lazzatti the strong young man he is today.
My interview included Daniel, Jennifer, and Cheryl, and
we began by having Daniel retell his story. I knew it would
be more detailed because of the limits of television time,
and I knew I had a number of facts that had to be checked
thoroughly. Here's the story of how Daniel Lazzatti gar-
nered my vote as the "Toughest Kid in America."

Middle school teachers and counselors began to notice
some problems with Daniel's behavior the previous six or
seven years. His parents were still married, but they were in
a seemingly constant struggle. Daniel tried to recall when
his mother eventually left and could pin it down to either
seventh or eighth grade. She had her fill of the father's crack
addiction and decided that it was best to leave the unit.

Now, there was an unusual financial issue that appeared because the family owned their house outright. Because of the impending divorce, the house had to be sold, and that was accomplished when a developer moved in and delivered the cash so that his mom could have her half and split. His dad received custody of Daniel and his brother, and the plan was to stay in the house and pay the developer some rent. Interesting problems came in hordes because his father wasn't working, and the only income he had was from collecting and recycling aluminum cans. Ouch!

The next four months after his mother left were described by Daniel as "carefree times." That was because the developer told his dad and brothers that they didn't have to pay rent while the family dispute lingered. Eventually, his brother moved out to be with the mother in another town, and time moved on. Eventually, the rent did have to be paid, and his father did it for a while. Then he just "stopped paying the rent." Hurricane season came, major damage occurred, and Dad believed that he would be receiving money from FEMA. What a surprise—it never happened. Eventually the family got evicted by the developer and the police. They were told they had twenty minutes to gather all their things and get out.

What would you do in those circumstances? What did they do? Within hours, they broke back into their old house. Daniel and his father lived there *undiscovered* for two months. The power was never turned off. The cable still functioned. It was two months on the lam. Then they were discovered and re-evicted, and Daniel Lazzatti hit a bit of a wall emotionally. Dad wanted to pull off Sneak

Back Two, the Revenge, but Daniel grabbed his stuff and left for good. When I asked what he was thinking at that very moment, he replied, "Nothing. Just get out."

At this point, another family knew of Daniel Lazzatti's situation and said he could spend the night with them to sort out a game plan. His father dropped him off at their house and said he would back to get him. He never returned.

That one-night stay turned into a long-term relationship, and the plan emerged for Daniel to prepare the tool shed out back for his new domicile. He didn't have a car at his disposal, so he searched the local Dumpsters and found a discarded child's bike. He rode it everywhere for two years, even though it didn't have any brakes. Daniel showered in the main house and did his laundry there once every week. But his house was the old tool shed and it seemed to me that's the way he wanted it. Oh by the way, I did not notice any electricity or running water in the shed, only a mattress on cinder blocks. His graduation robe still hangs on the wall where the rake used to hang.

The food issue was tough. Daniel received some donated restaurant food left over at the end of the day, and his dad would bring by some of his cache. In fact, today Dad still lives somewhere in the neighborhood *in a tent*. The biggest food score was after one of Florida's infamous hurricane hits. Power had been lost, stores had to discard expired food, and he had access to an old station wagon that didn't run. He recalled filling the car with "Twinkies, cookies, and vanilla wafers." He "feasted" for the next six months. Danny recalls this as a high moment. Food was aplenty.

But the really important part of the story is how he

valued his education and did what he could to maximize his efforts to succeed in that process. When I asked him why he didn't go down the wrong path of life and why he chose to excel in spite of the crappy cards dealt to him, he said, "I didn't lose everything. I still had family. I still had clothes on my back. Why should I go down the other path? And not only that, I'm doing so well in school. Why should I let that wither away?"

## His Educational Values

Daniel Lazzatti is a special case for sure. Here's a kid that had nothing but the clothes on his back and a Dumpster bike. And yet he valued his education almost more than anything in the world. I asked him why.

"It's just fun. I just enjoy it—the fascination of just learning. It was more important than saying, 'Let's get a house.'" He noted that he would rather live "under a bridge," get up every day, and go to school than just work to have a roof over his head. That's an unusual set of values for today's Americans.

Recall that I mentioned he came to Edgewater High School as a special education ninth grader. In the state of Florida, there is a different diploma awarded to kids in exceptional services programs. Daniel didn't want that degree; he wanted the traditional one. So he approached his two counselors at the end of his freshman year and decided to go for the real diploma. Now he had to squeeze four years of courses into his remaining three years—with a learning disability. That meant he would have to go to night school in addition to his daytime load of now more rigorous courses. He did that (including two periods of Geometry per day) and finished with that 3.7 GPA I talked about earlier.

Here's some key advice from Mr. Lazzatti to today's high school kids:

> "Go to school, learn something, and have some fun."

What follows is a segment of my interview with Daniel that turned up some other gems of strength in his personality.

"Are you religious?"

*"No way. Sunday was the 'National Gorge Your Face Day' at the Chinese Buffet."*

Did he ever have the chance to become religious? It is important to note that he did not have a faith system there to rely on. He truly was on an island.

"Have you ever thought about life being unfair?"

*"Sometimes, but I never use it."*

"What's physically the hardest thing you've ever done?"

*"Running in the rain when my bike was stolen."*

In the spring of his senior year, things turned around for Daniel. He was becoming mildly famous and admired for his exploits of independence. Someone had given him a newer bike, and it was a major upgrade from the Dumpster bike.

One morning in March, he walked out to ride to school and discovered the new bike had been stolen. He remembered having one response, *"Oh man, this is going to be hard to do."*

Rather than just call the school and tell them he wouldn't be able to be there, he found some plastic grocery sacks to cover his backpack. Why? Because it was raining, and he *had* to get to school. So he ran to school. When I asked the counselors how far that was, they weren't sure. Their best guess was between three and six miles. It took him a little over an hour to do it, and I later drove the distance in my rental car. It was close to six miles. *"One thing I've learned to do is dry stuff."*

"Talk about taking Geometry twice a day. Did you do it for better understanding?"

*"Nobody loves Geometry. I only like it."*

Daniel did attend two periods each day for better understanding and also because the second one was an honors section. He got to see some new stuff that he wouldn't have otherwise seen. It is another indicator that he likes to learn.

"Where did you do your daily homework? In school or in the shed?"

Danny Lazzatti developed a great habit. He would do his homework before he left school if it was at all possible. He found he could concentrate better at school than in the shed.

"You didn't have a job until this spring, and now you have two. Why didn't you have one earlier?"

*"Nobody would hire me. I either didn't have experience, or I wasn't yet eighteen."* He says he has two

jobs now because he likes to work. I think he just likes to live.

"Where are you living today?"

This was a cool answer. As Daniel's situation became better known, someone stepped forward and donated an apartment (free of charge) for his current living situation.

The donor probably did it without even getting a tax write-off.

In the final minutes of the interview, I asked Daniel what advice he would give to other students about taking care of oneself, and in the case of the parents, advice for raising their kids.

For students, his advice is:

*"Always stick to your values ... avoid peer pressure. Whatever you are pursuing, go for it."*

*"You really shouldn't do that [go against regulations]. You are wasting people's time. This [high school] is where it really counts—because it's free."*

*"Education is not for everybody. Follow your dreams, and do almost whatever you have to do to get where you are going."*

"What advice would you have for parents?"

*"I would tell them it's okay to spoil your kid ... but only once in a blue moon."*

*"If they ask for thirty dollars, ask them why ... "*

*"Always stick by their sides, to an extent ... "*

So that's arguably the toughest kid in America. Let me get one thing clear right now—Daniel Lazzatti is tougher than my kids were, and there's no way your kids will ever approach that level either. The fact is, nobody wants their child to go through the early life Daniel did.

But Daniel Lazzatti proves a major point of mine: it is possible for today's children to become independent, reliable, and responsible. If your kid is too soft, or if he or she is heading in that direction, it is possible to help them acquire more toughness. Like Daniel, someday soon they will be on their own.

*They have to be able to take care of themselves. In a perfect world, every child would reach for the top of the food pyramid. People are like all other organisms. Organisms at the top get to choose their pathways in life.*

# Tough Kids First

Here is the meat of the issue. I have seen two distinct groups of kids emerge from the masses as we speak. Some kids are still mentally solid, "tough," if you will. They still have that tradition-based, great work ethic; they can manage their own issues with organizational skills that are becoming well honed, and they have the ability to solve their own problems when they arise. These kids didn't just emerge; they've been raised this way. Their parents deserve major kudos. I'll identify some specific examples of quality parenting for you in a later chapter. Also, I think my survey results will convince you that kids today really want that kind of parenting.

There is another group of children that seem to be struggling in comparison. These youngsters may not be totally irresponsible, but they live in a gray fog; sometimes they are getting the job done, sometimes not. With this group, there is still time to salvage the behaviors and skills that they need to move up to our first group. This is the group I'm targeting. *The bottom line is that you want your kid to grow to be a successful adult, one that can function successfully in an independent life that he or she is in control of.*

Do we see evidence of these kids failing to get to the stated goal? Witness one statistic and ask yourself a major societal question, "Would you, today's parent, want to raise your kid's kids?"

In 1970, 2.2 million children were being raised in "grand-parent-maintained" settings, and by the year 2000, the number of American children in this situation had grown to 4.4 million (Census 1970, Census 2000). The number of kids living in this tough situation doubled in thirty years. So who's next in line to be raising kids instead of living the golden life they've earned? Making your kids mentally tough will help you avoid having to raise *their* kids.

"Softness begets softness. Turn this mush around."

Here's a group of high school students and their behaviors that I've seen over the course of the last thirty years. I'm going to start with the positive ones, characteristics that I think every person would admire in their child. These young men and young women have done some impressive things that merit their belonging to the top group of "mentally tough" kids.

## Admire These Kids—Toughness Rules

Michelle C. (PHS Class of 1981) and
Stacy K. (PHS Class of 1983)

Michelle and Stacy do not even know each other. They had totally separate experiences here at Pomona, and yet through my eyes, both of them brought similar qualities that bear noting in this book. Later I have a chapter dedicated to the "Four Keys to Success." These two women exemplified what you want your kid to look like in the arena of "Key Number Three: Maximize Your Efforts."

Michelle was one of my Chemistry kids during the years that our school was on a year-round type of schedule called Concept Six. Our system had a quarter-based system rather than semesters, so we provided grades four times a year, rather than the traditional two-semester system we are currently on. Even though there was much shuffling of students throughout the year, I had Michelle for all four quarters and saw an incredible amount of development and improvement throughout that course of time.

Here's the essence of Michelle C's academic profile in the area of high school science classes:

As a first quarter Chemistry student, she received a very low C for the nine weeks. College Prep Chemistry is very difficult stuff, and she was struggling with the challenge. It was not a matter of lack of effort; it was just a difficult course for her. She was really frustrated with how close she came to receiving a D.

As a second quarter Chemistry student, Michelle faced a new challenge. Even though she was dedicated to bumping up her grade, the material was going to get more difficult. That's the nature of how our course is designed. Even though science was not "her thing," it was clear that Ms. C was going to try to raise that grade.

She came very close to receiving a B for the quarter, but it didn't happen; it was a high C. Now at this point in time, it would have been real easy for Michelle to quit the program, and I'm betting that she thought about it. There was, however, something ingrained in her personality that just would not let her do it. She registered for the rest of the year.

Third and fourth quarter Chemistry are running at an accelerated pace, and it's more than fair to say it becomes pretty difficult. For those of you familiar with the subject, we cover kinetics, thermodynamics, equilibrium, acid-base chemistry, and redox. Even if these terms mean nothing, they *sound* tough and are really hard to pronounce and spell. Trust me, the course gets difficult. Michelle dug in like a mole. She began to envision the abstract material better, and her effort level and determination were first rate. She finished the quarter with a solid B.

The final quarter was here (we used to call it Chemistry D), and I noticed a new confidence in Michelle. Was she more confident because of the B a few days earlier? Probably. Maybe I gave her the B just to motivate her and build a sense of confidence for the final nine weeks. Probably not. That's just not my style. She earned it, and without a doubt, I was excited for her. The point is, she earned it. Michelle C. finished the final quarter with a low A because of a total mixture of tail-busting effort and increased self-confidence on her part. She believed she could conquer the subject, and she did.

------

Stacy K. was a totally different story. She was a quiet young lady in high school and always had a major determination in academics and how they should be approached. She, unlike Michelle, was always ranked near the top of her class and finished with a class rank in the top ten in 1983. I think it's fair to say that math and science classes always made a bit more sense naturally to Stacy than they did to Michelle. Stacy showed her mental toughness in unique ways, just like Michelle did.

Upon graduation, Ms. K. entered an engineering school in New Mexico (New Mexico Tech) in the fall of 1983. Even though she was an excellent high school student and really talented in the fields of math and science, she found that place to be a major challenge. It presented a vehicle to reach a great long-term goal—get a quality job in engineering and achieve the rewards that go with it. It wasn't going to be easy. In fact, the oil industry was in a definite downturn, and only three students in her class got those quality jobs. Guess what. They were the kids with the three highest grade point averages (Stacy's was a meteoric 3.4 overall).

Additionally, she was entering a domain that has traditionally been dominated by males throughout time. Lots of cards were stacked against her, and maybe even today that's still true. Harvard's past president, Lawrence H. Summers, recently suggested that females may fall behind in math and the sciences because they don't have the same "innate ability" as males for those fields (*Boston Globe*—January 17, 2005) In Stacy's world, that attitude problem was even bigger in the fall of 1983.

So What Happened to Michelle and Stacy?

Michelle C., originally limited in the sciences, continued her practice of strong-willed work ethic, attended a high-quality university in the southwest, and became a practicing architect. She's still doing it today and has achieved a number of accomplishments in a field that she loves. Without her mentally tough approach, none of that would have happened.

Stacy K. acquired her degree in petroleum engineering and currently works for an independent oil company in America. She makes a lot of money: like hundreds of thousands of American dollars. She has made the final call on a giant oil field acquisition for a previous employer while only sleeping three hours per night. How big was the call? It was 1.5 billion dollars big. That's with a B. Lawrence Summers didn't know Stacy K., and like Michelle, mental toughness worked wonders for Stacy.

Learn This from Michelle and Stacy: "Nothing is more important for success than maximizing your efforts."

## Anthony Randall (Class of 1993)

Anthony Randall was one of the most unique students I've ever had. He was a pretty good high school Chemistry student, but what really made him memorable was the way he approached the start of class every day. He would come to class and be pumping himself up right before the starting bell. I remember a consistent, light, double-fisted rhythmic pounding of his desk and the perpetual question, "Hey, Mr. Smiley, are we going to blow something up today?" Chemistry kids love the sensational demonstrations they occasionally see, but Anthony expected one every day.

Even though Mr. Randall was a consistent treat of enthusiasm on a daily basis, he was also a very determined student, inquisitive by nature, and blessed with only pretty fair innate ability. He had to scratch for everything he understood, and many afternoons or early mornings were spent going over some of the finer points of electron orbital theory or chemical equilibrium conditions. I always liked his willingness to know when to get help by walking into my room after hours.

After he left high school, he headed for the U.S. Military Academy at West Point, and I believed his work ethic would fit him well in his new environment. What I didn't know was how rough the next few years would become for him.

Anthony, like a number of young men and women, had a tough go at West Point.

Anthony recently described some of his experiences. "It's a culture shock. On the first day an officer walked in and said, 'Ladies and gentlemen, today all of your freedoms and liberties have been taken away. They are given back as a privilege.'"

I know what we're all thinking. *Hey, it's a military academy.* While this is true, few eighteen-year-olds are ready for that kind of environment. Many people think it builds a lot of character, and you can count Anthony among them. Even though he would tell you that West Point had a positive influence on his being, Anthony ran into a virtual buzz saw of controversy during his sophomore year at the academy.

The military academies in the U.S. operate on a strong basis of self-integrity for its students and future officers. If you are involved in a cheating situation or other integrity violation, you are expected to turn yourself in. Likewise, if you even know of it going on, you are committed to turning in the violators, who could even be your best friends. This is a major step up for many of the students at places like West Point, and the system even goes a step further.

Anthony Randall was working with some classmates one evening and thought they were studying for an upcoming exam. Students are allowed to view old exams and work with one another in a cooperative fashion. Anthony thought that was the nature of the work one evening when, in fact, his roommate had stolen the answer key for the upcoming exam. A few days later, his roommate's instructor approached Anthony's roommate for cheating.

Even though Anthony was unaware of the incident, he had to turn himself in for "tolerating" the incident. That's part of the self-report system used at the academy. What transpired next wasn't right, but it was a severe twist in Anthony Randall's life for an extended period of time.

Rumors fly in life, and as we all know, they are totally inaccurate many times. The word got out that Anthony had turned the others in and that he was the one that had actually cheated. He received a number of threats of physical violence, and his room was vandalized. His physical existence was threatened, and he had to live with the dark cloud for a number of weeks. Eventually, he was attacked and a physical event took place with a number of individuals involved on both sides of the support train for Anthony. The originally accused offenders were expelled three weeks after the original scam.

Anthony Randall saw his grades plummet during this time and barely cut a 2.0 GPA for the semester. He eventually arose from the ashes, and finished his career that took off after graduation. How many of us could have been as strong?

### So What Happened to Anthony?

I remember starting one of my Chemistry classes in the late 1990s (I think it was third period) in a traditional way on a traditional day. I was asking the class to figure out one of the logic problems I give twice a week (called Deviant Thinker's Questions), when I looked up and saw Anthony standing in the back of my class wearing his military uniform. Needless to say, I was a bit stunned but immediately reacted by saying "Hey, Anthony, welcome back to the world of high school Chemistry. So what are you doing these days?"

He responded with a statement that vividly rings today. "Mr. Smiley, I became a demolitions expert at West Point. There's not a bridge in the world today I can't take down." Remember that he wanted to blow up something every day in his high school Chemistry class. At least he focused that passion in a positive arena by working for his country.

I lost track of Anthony for a few years after his surprise visit, but I came to learn of other amazing feats he attained by the time he was in his early thirties. He became an Army Ranger to do his military work at a higher level than ever before, became injured in a particular parachute maneuver, and left the military a few years ago. He then took his massive energy to the private sector and became a very successful entrepreneur.

Anthony Randall stopped by in my classroom in the spring of 2005 and presented me with a copy of his new book, *The Vanguard Factor.*

The latest news was that he had spent the last three years in a seminary, where he has become an ordained minister. Anthony recently re-enlisted in the army to serve his fellow soldiers as a chaplain. In January 2008, Anthony Randall was in Iraq working with our young men and women there in a very difficult area. I don't know of another case where any young person has accomplished so many different things at such a young age.

Learn this from Anthony: "Perseverance and energy can carry you to great heights."

## Chris V.E. (Class of 1998)

I have known Chris V.E. since he was a pretty young guy—maybe late elementary school. I had known his older brother and sister earlier because they were in my science classes during their high school years. Additionally, Momma V.E. had been my sons' elementary school teacher. The two families knew each other pretty well. But

I had no idea how well I would come to know Chris as an athlete, a student (one of top ones I've seen), and as a high-quality young man.

Mr. V.E. was a mediocre young athlete, but it was readily apparent by seventh grade that he was going to be a pretty big mammal. At that time he was tall, a bit overweight, and pretty slow running down the basketball court—really nothing special as a player. As a coach, you realize and hope that things will change for a kid like that in the next few years, and sure enough, it did for Chris. My next set of encounters with Chris was when he entered high school in the fall of 1994. Oddly enough, I became the head basketball coach in the fall of 1995. He finished his basketball career as one of Pomona High School's all-time great players.

How did Chris's basketball career progress over the four-year period? I can only give you secondhand information about his freshman year, but believe me, it was pretty uneventful. He was a third-string player at best, as we say in the business, "Riding the pine."

The best story of Chris V.E.'s freshman season goes down to a game late in the season when the coach walked down to the end of the bench for some unknown reason. Maybe it was to put the "big kid" in the game. What Coach Mackin found was really unbelievable. Chris V.E. was powering down some Twinkies while he passed his time on the bench. I've never seen a player eating anything on any bench. But I guess now we have a handle on why he did not yet have a chiseled body.

As a sophomore, Mr. V.E. grew to about six foot five, and he became more athletic. Interestingly enough, there was another sophomore player on the level three team that was very similar. These two guys represented Coach Mackin's "big men," and both showed some promise for their final two years. Mid-way through the season, the team lost a close game that they should have won, and Coach M. was really frustrated and upset.

Now, Danny Mackin was a very young assistant coach of mine but also very bright and adaptable to what a team needed. As we discussed the game, my comment was that his team was way too slow when he played both of his big guys simultaneously. I said, "Here's the new policy, Danny. Either Chris or James is in the game, but never together. Pit them against each other in practice and let them know that the best man in practice will get the largest share of the game time minutes. Let's find out who the most competitive kid is."

It was stunning to see what happened next. Chris's abilities and efforts rose like a kite in a high wind. James sank like a rock. Within a few weeks, we knew that Chris V.E. was going to be a major player for the next two years. James quit the program.

Chris grew to six foot seven and created 235 pounds of muscle with a phenomenal effort in the weight room over the next twenty-four months. He became an all-state 5A player and went on to Columbia University in New York to play basketball and develop his intellect. He gradu-ated from high school as his class valedictorian, hit some meteoric SAT scores, and graduated from Columbia with a degree in four years, majoring in mathematics with a computer science minor. What is he doing today, at age twenty-seven? He lives in San Francisco as a financial consultant. He has multiple certifications that you only get if you're really smart and work really hard. I think he works too many hours, and we talk about that every time we have a meal when he gets back to Denver. I don't know how much money he makes, but it's in the neighborhood of $300,000 annually. Eleven years earlier he was eating Twinkies during a basketball game.

It's important to understand this about Chris: the large amount of money he makes is really secondary to what he is about. He became very tough mentally through the continual challenges he accepted as an athlete and as a scholar. He became the *consummate* team player. Those are qualities that he uses every day in his new life.

What if Chris had not accepted the challenges put forth to him as a sophomore basketball player? He could have thought it was too hard. He could have thought it was unfair and then asked his parents to call the coach and complain. He did neither. He took care of his problem and of himself. Today, he's like granite.

Learn this from Chris: "Never fear the challenge. Hard work always wins out."

## Kyle O. (Class of 2000)

Kyle is the most impressive young man I've ever taught. He's also one of the most inspirational. In the fall of 1999, Kyle was a senior in one of my college preparatory Chemistry classes. He seemed like a nice kid, sat in the front row of the room (left side, near the fume hood) and just seemed like your prototypical Pomona kid of the last twenty-five years. I had no clue how special he was.

The fall semester was proceeding along in a normal fashion, and as usual, I began to know my students a bit better with each passing week. I noticed that Kyle was a good student (probably an A student at the end of the semester), and that he was willing to participate strongly in all of our class discussions on a daily basis. I also noticed that Kyle seemed a bit sluggish, if you will, but I couldn't really put my finger on why.

A few more weeks slid by, and he informed me that he was a severe epileptic. He told me that he would have numerous severe seizures every week, and that because of that, he couldn't drive a car, play sports, etc. I had never seen another kid with the affliction to that degree. I found out that his sluggish characteristics were caused by the type and quantity of medication he had to take to control his seizures. It then became clear that what I was really seeing was kind of a "doped up" Kyle O. on a daily basis. His eyes were a bit droopy, kind of like he was always a bit sleepy, and his speech might have been slightly slurred. Nonetheless, he was always a positive guy in the class-room, and he did finish the semester with an A.

I began to realize how special Kyle was during the fall semester when he was finishing a class period one day with something unusual on his desk. I noticed two large (eleven-by-fourteen) pieces of paper that were filled with typed columns of Latin words in a programmed sequence. It clearly took a long time to create this "data" and a substantial effort to just mechanically type it up. I was more than a little bit curious, so I asked him what this was.

He replied, "I have a Latin quiz next period, so I made this study sheet for it." He wasn't even going to turn this creation in! My next statement was made in jest when I said, "So what's this quiz worth? 1,000 points?"

Kyle's response was very matter-of-fact. "No, only about ten to fifteen points."

This was a kid making an ultimate effort, probably the biggest I've ever seen for such a small quantitative reward. He was doing it simply because it was the right thing to do to prepare himself for success in his Latin class. I've since laminated those sheets, and they hang on a special wall in my classroom (see these in the photo gallery at the back of the book).

It was getting fairly late in the fall semester when I began my instructional day with a six thirty a.m. help session for the test I was giving later that day. About eighty kids would take that test, and around thirty of them were in the voluntary help session that morning.

We work all kinds of problems, answer any questions they want, etc., until seven fifteen, and then the faucet is shut off. Once the first exam goes off at seven thirty, I do not answer any more questions. If a student wants to get some help, they must make it in by six thirty, or forever hold their peace. This is done for a couple of reasons, one of which is to make sure we promote *ultimate effort* on the students' parts.

Kyle was in the back of the room, working problems on the board with the others, when I heard a kid say, "Hey, Mr. Smiley. Kyle's having a seizure." I whipped around from the board at the front of the room and saw that Kyle had fallen out of his desk and was lying on his side on the floor, beginning to have the seizure. We cleared everything out of his way and let him go through the process. My other students were a bit freaked out, to say the least. The seizure lasted for about ninety seconds.

I don't think I can adequately describe what happened next, but it taught me a huge life lesson about effort levels and how you need to deal with adversity in your life.

As Kyle O. came back to consciousness, I tried to communicate with him to see how he was doing. I asked him if he was okay. He said he was and then, without any further statement, *he literally climbed back into his desk and finished the problem that was on the board.* No one else in the room (myself included) could say anything. I just watched as a young guy dealt with his everyday life.

## So What Happened to Kyle?

Kyle had cutting-edge brain surgery during the spring of his senior year in high school, and great things eventually happened for him. The surgery eliminated his physiological problem. He was weaned off most of his medications (it took about a year to do this), and he started to live an unaffected life as a college student. I saw him a couple of times in the last few years, and he looked fantastic.

He hasn't had a seizure since, and he has acquired a driver's license, lost about thirty pounds of excess weight, and told me a few years ago that he was running five miles every day because "it just really felt good" to do it. *Even though his life had taken a really positive turn, it's important to remember that Kyle was just as positive in his life attitude before the surgery as he is today.*

P.S.—On an incredibly sad note—Kyle Ordway died on July 4, 2006 in his sleep at the age of twenty-four He had completed all of his coursework to receive his masters in engineering. He was unbelievably accomplished regardless of his shortcomings. I leave you with one quote from Kyle on his memorial card at the funeral:

> "Never quit, never give up; for today is a new light, and tomorrow shall bring another chance for happiness and joy."

Learn this from Kyle: "No matter what cards you are dealt in life, handle them in a positive fashion."

## Benny G. (Class of 2006)

Ben is living proof that there is hope for today's youth. He was a senior in one of my Chemistry classes in the fall of 2005, and he's shown way more toughness than I thought he had when he first walked through the door in August. Now understand something very clearly: I was betting that Ben couldn't finish the job. So what was his job in my class?

Ben was one of my first hour Chemistry students, and he began the year with what I call "the affliction." First hour begins at seven twenty-five a.m., and some students struggle mightily with being on time at that point in the day. I've used a variety of techniques to emphasize the need to be timely, and I think I exhausted the entire arsenal on

Ben. Even though I encouraged, counseled, berated, and ripped on Ben, he kept pulling the tardy card, and yet he always apologized.

This whole thing went on for about the first six weeks of school, and then something monumental occurred. Ben came in and said, "Hey, Mr. Smiley, I'm not going to miss class anymore, and I promise that I won't be tardy either."

My response went something like this, "Hey, Ben, don't make promises you can't keep." He continued to say, "No, I mean it this time, and in fact, I'll bet you it doesn't happen anymore." I responded, "Hey, Bennie, I can't take your money, but the loser could buy the other guy a steak dinner." He agreed, and the rest of the story is history. He won the wager, and I was down about $100. Only twice did Benny G. come close to blowing the bet, and they were classics.

Six weeks into the wager came one October morning when it looked like he was headed for the toaster. The clock was only about twenty seconds from exterminating Ben when the door blasted open, and the kid dove in the doorway. He was lying on the floor and looked like he'd been hit by a bus. When I asked him what's up, Ben informed us that his alarm failed to go off, and he had only been awake for the last seven minutes. What? He lives at least five minutes away by car, and that means he had to jump out of bed, jump in his car, and then drive to school. I think the only way he could possibly have pulled this off was to park his car on the lawn and then sprint to class. He literally had less than one minute to make it.

About two weeks later, he had another close call with the "Grim Reaper Clock" of room 421. He had begun to soften when he didn't realize that he had to scrape his windshield before he left for school on a frosty Thursday morning. It cost him about three extra minutes, traffic was bad getting into the parking lot, and it took a full-blown sprint from his car to my class to make it by about fifteen seconds. I'm guessing it may have been a world record for the quarter mile. On both occasions, Ben received ovations from his classmates.

There's a huge lesson for all of us when viewing Benny G.'s success. He was able to keep his promise by prioritizing timeliness in his life. I know the kid wanted the steak dinner, but it really was bigger than that. How did his grades in my class fare during the wager? At the beginning, Ben had a solid B, and by the end of the semester he had turned that into a solid A.

Have you read some of the new educational research that says kids would be better learners if we started high school classes after nine a.m? I refuse to even cite this garbage. If you want to assume that it's okay for kids to go to sleep at two a.m. or later, then I suppose it could be valid. But then tell me this. How many quality jobs in America begin the workday at nine a.m. or later? Haven't we all heard about the overzealous American work system that starts earlier and ends later than any other country in the world? How are we going to prepare kids to become productive adults if they don't have the ability to crank it up early in the day? Kids need sleep. Make them go to bed at a reasonable time.

Learn this from Ben: "You can accomplish anything— if it's a priority."

## Monica T. (Class of 2007)

The fall of 2007 introduced me to a really high-quality young lady. Monica T. had both my Field Geology class and one of my college preparatory Chemistry classes in her schedule. I had heard from one of our Physics teachers that she was really "rock solid," but that could mean a lot of things to different eyes. I discovered mid-way through the semester what Mr. K. had meant.

I typically take a few weeks to get to know my students and really try to not rush to judgment on any of them. Some turn out to be much better than I thought and some turn out to be, well, less than the first impression. Monica was riding along about like I had heard, and so no surprises seemed to be coming. She seemed to be *only* rock solid.

Field Geology is a course I teach as part of our Science Seminar program here at Pomona. The philosophy of the entire program is to involve our top science students in courses that have them doing science on a daily basis rather than just taking another text and lecture class. These classes replace an AP science program but operate at the college level daily. Four of these courses (including Field Geology) receive college credit from the University of Colorado system. Students are encouraged to become better thinkers and more independent than they are accustomed to. Monica felt the strain at the halfway point of the semester.

The class is based on weekly field trips where the students collect real-world data on Mondays and then typically map and analyze the data in the lab during the rest of the week. The largest project involves an entire weekend on top of Vail Pass in the Colorado Rockies, where the class members create two original topographic maps. Sophisticated equipment like Brunton compasses, GPS units, and digital altimeters are in their hands like scientific weapons. One map is done by essentially "old school" methodologies, while the other uses the newest technology. The actual creation of the maps occurs in the lab for the next three weeks, and it challenges the finest students to the maximum every year.

Three weeks flew by, and we arrived at the final Friday before Black Monday (when everything was due), and very few of the kids were feeling totally confident coming into the final stretch. Monica was in a unique position because she felt like there was a major problem with the project.

Nearly a month had been dedicated to solving the mystery, and Ms. T received a giant dose of "Oh, no!" with about fifty hours to go. A major error was discovered, and I even felt a bit sorry for her as she left the class on Friday afternoon. I was pretty sure that she would make a rock-solid effort to save the ship by Monday. I really didn't give her enough credit, in retrospect.

As Monday, 1:00 p.m. arrived, the students delivered the goods, and Monica was looking a bit tired but relieved as she turned it in. I remember asking her how it went, and she responded in the affirmative. Five days later, I arrived at grading her maps, and I was stunned. *Not only had she survived, but Monica's maps were clearly the best of the entire group.* Now remember, these were the best science kids in the school, and no matter what spin is placed on it, it's a competitive process. Monica T. had achieved the mountaintop when a couple of days earlier, she was in a "crash and burn" mode. How had she come so far, so fast?

## Two Factors—Maximum Effort and Maximum Self-Confidence

One weekend had seen a minimum of fifteen hours of her time. It might be more. Maybe she lost track. However, none of it would have been possible if she had not believed that it was possible. *Parents need to create this attitude in their kids.* Monica T. is proof positive that great kids and great students with toughness can exist in the world today. Help your kids become determined and tough like Monica T.

Learn this from Monica: "It doesn't matter if you get knocked down—how long will it take to get back up?"

As a parent, you should be asking yourself this question. *Which of the previous students would be best for my son or daughter to model?*

# I'm a Bit Soft—
# I Need Some Help

Here we go now. That's enough of the pie-in-the-sky kids. While there are more really great examples of solid work ethic out there, I contend there are many more that are sliding the slippery slope. I've also said that the issue resides around how they have been raised. As you read this section, realize that you are the objective observer, and I'm not talking about *your* kid here. Or am I? I'm going to begin with a few illustrations, and I want you to try to remain objective. Realize that these are real kids with real stories.

We begin with two of my own past students. Parent reactions are included, so you can get a full picture of the whole event. I'll let you judge for yourself whether or not they acted/reacted appropriately to their kid's behavior.

## Billy X. (Eleventh Grader, Spring of 2004)

In the beginning, I mentioned there was an incident where I kind of snapped and told one of my classes, "That's it. I'm writing a book." Theoretical Billy is the kid that made me go over the edge. Thanks, Billy, I needed it.

Billy was a Chemistry student in my first period class during the spring semester, and he began to have some major issues with getting to class on time. If you haven't figured it out yet, that's a big issue in my view. Now don't get me wrong, Billy was a nice kid. He had what started as a minor problem, but by April it was "big time."

He stayed after class one morning, and I asked young William why he was always either late or just absent altogether. To his credit, he was honest with me and said, "Hey, Mr. S, I just can't seem to wake up, and so sometimes I don't make it here until second hour."

In the old days of high school education, administrators had the desire and district backing to lean hard on kids in the area of attendance. There were years when the district had specific limits on the number of absences and/or tardies a kid could acquire before credit would be withheld. As time has gone on for the last fifteen or twenty years, *our society has softened up*; parents have acquired lawyers, etc., and leaned on school boards and superintendents to the point where the administration feels hamstrung on taking a hard stand. Teachers can be left out on a limb (one of our administrations was infamous for that) to deal with the problem themselves. I'm personally all right with that because I relish the chance to change the youngster's bad habits. But all teachers do not see it that way, nor should they. *Strong administrators should make decisions that help students, not hurt them.*

So back to Billy. When he told me that he was oversleeping, I replied, "How can that be? All of these tardies and absences are called in as *excused* absences." Billy got a bit quiet and said, "I ask my dad to call in the excuses for them."

Now fast forward to that afternoon when I got a chance to call Billy's dad at his workplace. The conversation went like this:

> "Hey, Mr. X, this is Mr. Smiley at Pomona. I'm Billy's Chemistry teacher first hour. I'm having a problem with his attendance in that he's either not here or frequently late."
>
> Mr. X says, "Oh yeah, he has a really tough time waking up. I have a hard time getting him out of bed."
>
> I thought, *Are you kidding me? This guy is unable to get Billy up, and instead of having a consequence hanging for Billy when he oversleeps, this guy calls our attendance system with a fake excuse.*
>
> My response was, "Well, now I'm really confused, Mr. X, because all of these problems are called in as excused occurrences."
>
> Mr. X says, "Yeah well, he asked me to do that for him."
>
> I said, "Do you have any clue how badly you are hurting Billy by doing that?"
>
> Silence.
>
> My final comment was, "Sir, I really expect there will be no more of these calls.

Billy was in class without incident for the final six weeks. Why? I'm sure Dad stepped up and laid out an expectation on his son, and there was probably an implied consequence. Nice job, Dad. Just do it sooner.

Learn this from Billy and his dad: "Common sense reactions with expectations pay big time."

## Wanda K. (Senior, Fall of 2004)

The issue of parental judgment can intensify. My second example of softness involves a new phenomenon in today's parental attitudes: "I'll go on vacation when I want to, and it shouldn't affect my kid's grade."

Wow. Where and when did this come from? The example of Ms. Wanda K. is, I think, stunning but not atypical. Here it is.

Wanda was a senior during the fall semester of 2004 and reputed to be a very good student. My experience with her in Chemistry began with her doing well early on. Now for those of you that remember your high school chemistry experiences, you probably recall that it's a pretty stout course. Ours is designed to start at a little bit slower pace and then to begin to accelerate. By the end of the first semester, the class is on fire. As I said, Wanda did well early on.

With about a month to go in the semester (early November), Wanda came to inform me that she was going to go to Italy for about ten days with a friend. I responded in the kids' vernacular and said, "Sup?" She then explained that the trip was a vacation and that her parents were not going, but she had her mother's full backing.

My response was to try to discourage the trip because we were getting into tougher waters in the course, and missing ten days was going to cause her to drop in the grading world. I remember her exact response. "It's okay. I'll make it up when I get back." The problem often is more complicated than that. The student misses class time, lab time, and general understanding of the material. The thing to remember here is that this is a kid that wants to do well and will probably be unhappy if she does not.

Wanda came back from Italy, worked hard to make up the work that she missed, took the test, and received a 72 percent. Not bad in some areas, but she clearly desired an A for the semester, and so this began to put her behind the proverbial eight ball. As we neared the end of the semester, Wanda had accumulated an 87 percent cumulative total, when 90 percent was the minimum for an A. One more fact worked in her favor. I have one extra credit opportunity available during each semester, and it was coming up soon. Wanda came to the 6:00 a.m. session, worked for the extra hour, and received nineteen extra credit points. This brought her extremely close to the A line. Crunch time was approaching.

Wanda came to see me the day before the final and asked, "Mr. Smiley, do I have a chance at still getting an A in the class?" My response was, "Maybe. You're probably going to have to knock the final out cold to have that happen." So how did she do? Wanda scored seventy-five out of eighty-five on the final, and that equates to 88 percent.

Fireworks began the next day when Wanda came in, found out that the final grade was a B, and asked if she could do some *more* extra credit to get to the A. I said no, game over. Wanda became distraught and said that possible scholarships were gone and that she may not be able to afford school in the fall. I said, "I'm sorry, but I'm sure something can be worked out." She continued to press the issue and through her tears said, "You just don't understand how important this is." My response was understanding but factual. "Wanda, I told you that the trip to Italy was risky. That was the test (72 percent performance) that brought you down. You made a choice to go, and now it's costing you."

Christmas break followed, and when I returned, I was called to the principal's office to hear that her mom had written him a letter talking about how unfairly Wanda was treated. Wanda had also mentioned that I had questioned the family's finances (why would I?) and her mother did not understand why I wouldn't work with Wanda to do "some extra work" for the A. The principal informed me I had an e-mail waiting on the school's system, and I said, "I won't trade e-mails. I'll call her and try to set up a meeting." E-mail is not the place for this kind of a personal trial.

I talked to Wanda's mother later that morning and invited her to come in. She couldn't because she couldn't take any time off work. Here is a huge issue with her daughter, but she couldn't leave work. I then told her we needed to solve it over the phone—she agreed.

The final point is that Wanda got a B because she earned a B. She was only close to the A because of the gratuitous nineteen-point extra credit piece she was allowed to do. She got a B on the final. The parental perspective was along the lines of why young kids should always get a trophy in little league sports. Wanda should be allowed to work until the B morphed into an A. *This is not real. You get what you earn.* If you choose to go on a trip, it's probably going to cost you. If you are an adult, you get fired. If you are a kid, you may fail.

Wanda was and is a great kid. Parental attitudes have caused her softness. It may not be the kid's fault, but it is the kid's problem to deal with.

Learn this from Wanda and her mom: "Make a choice. Live with the consequences."

## Athletic Camps and Parents

Well now, I've opened with two examples of today's softness for a specific reason. They represent a growing trend in parental attitudes that are really dangerous for your kid. I know what you are thinking: "I would never do either one of those things." Maybe. Try to survey what you do on a daily basis from now on, and then compare your vision to the student survey results I have included in a later chapter. Your view may be different than your kid's. Let me give you an example of how the *parental view* and the *kid's view* may be radically different.

My son Steve is twenty-seven years old and currently has a busy life going on. He has finished his MBA in the Texas A&M system and is currently a men's head basketball coach at a junior college in the west. Steve has also been a college professor of international business at his previous college assignment. He is pretty accomplished, largely because of his work ethic that was established early in both his academic and athletic lives.

Steve runs a basketball skills school with former teammate Sundance Wicks, who is an assistant basketball coach at Northern Illinois University. These camps take place in the summer, and they have one focus for the mostly high school-aged kids. They want to teach the players how to work on their skills on their own at an intense pace. In short, the camp improves their work ethic as a player. The theory is that all athletes must be taught how to maximize their individual growth by turning up the intensity of their workouts—especially when there is no coach around.

In 2006, this specific three-day camp was near an end, when Steve's partner, Sunny, gathered the players together and asked them three questions. Like many youth athletic activities, there were a large number of the parents a short distance away from the huddle but certainly within earshot of the discussion. In fact, Sunny planned it that way.

Here are Sunny's questions for the players in his quest to help them develop their attitudes and abilities within the *team* sport of basketball.

"Question one: Would you, as a high school player, prefer to have experience A or experience B? (A) Personally average twenty-five points per game, be named an all-state player, and have your team get three wins for the season, or (B) personally average six points per game, not be even an all-conference player, and have your *team* win the state championship?

When asked, virtually all of the kids raise their hands to choose scenario B.

Sunny then asked a significant question.

"Question two: How many of your parents would prefer that you have experience A?"

A nearly unanimous set of hands went up again.

Why did those hands go up? You, Mom and Dad, really do care what kind of future your kid is going to have. Sometimes it may be that you care too much about it. You are playing a delicate game, and you need to go a course that gives your son or daughter the best chance for *long-term* success in life. I'm thinking you want to be the kind of grandparents that send their grandkids home at the end of the visit.

# Did That Really Happen?

I'm pretty determined to paint the most *accurate* picture I can about the state of suburban high school kids in America today. It would be really easy to just talk about my personal encounters with students in the past thirty years, but then you might think it's not really a generalized issue. So here, in this very chapter, I bring you some more examples from other backgrounds. My teaching colleagues have shared some of their experiences for this book, and as mentioned earlier, we live in a very typical middle-class suburban high school setting. These examples are very real, and pertinent to what's happening in the "Softening of America."

I'm going to refer to my colleagues by letter rather than name. Some of these incidents are extreme, and I would say some happen regularly. Do any of these parenting responses seem familiar to you personally? If so, think about what effect this is having on your own kids.

## Teacher A and "Plagiarism"

Teacher A is a very solid, no-nonsense kind of teacher who also knows how to get a great effort from her students on a daily basis. She teaches a variety of classes in our department, and this example comes from our advanced Science Seminar program. In fact, her class has just been recently accredited to receive college credit. I would call the coursework substantial and significant.

A young student plagiarized the major final paper through the use of the Internet, and Teacher A caught it. A number of other colleagues were called in to analyze the issue, and there was no dispute that it had occurred. Teacher A talked to the student, expressed her disappointment, and informed him that he would receive zero credit for the project.

The net result was that his grade would drop from an A for the semester to the much less desired C. There was a faction of our science faculty that felt that the resulting penalty was too lenient, but it was definitely Teacher A's call. How flagrant was his offense anyway? The student had directly printed a number of pages and charts directly from the Internet and then represented the work as his own.

The outcome of the teacher/student discussion was that the student acknowledged the offense and seemed to accept the impending penalty for his actions. It's too bad that the parents didn't see it that way. Mom called the next day to find out what had happened (I think most of us would have also called) and had a detailed discussion with the teacher. That call ended on a basis of fundamental understanding that the punishment was more than fair in light of the fact that total course credit could have been withheld. Dad was not as accepting of the results.

This whole incident occurred right before the two-week holiday break. All teachers and students look forward to this time with a positive attitude because it's a time for recharging everybody's batteries. Teacher A had the pleasure of receiving five phone calls from Dad during that time as he tried to work the angle that junior really had done nothing wrong from day one. It almost sounded like an attempted negotiation (Dad's a lawyer). When his powers of reasoning didn't sway Teacher A, he turned his attention to our administration to overturn the ruling. Luckily, they held their ground, and the incident eventually evaporated. What makes this incident so important anyway?

I'll tell you why this matters—it matters because the kid was *wrong*. An intelligent, educated parent tries to muscle out a more favored consequence for his kid. Why did he do that? Was it a power trip? Is Dad trying to win approval and/or the love of his child? Who knows. This was a perfect opportunity to let this young student sink a bit in the quicksand of his indiscretion. There comes a time to not throw him the life preserver. *A great lesson could have been learned without the kid being exterminated.*

## Teacher B and "the Midstream Vacation"

I've already talked about this a little earlier, and yet here's a very typical example of the disease. I really don't think parents are thinking about how the kid will be affected when they get those great "off-season rates."

The fact is, there is a new attitude appearing within the school setting in suburban America. It's called the mid-semester vacation, and it goes something like this, "Hey, Mr. Smiley, I won't be here next week." My response would typically be, "Sup?" The student would probably deal up the line that he would miss the next five to ten days because the parents got a great price on a midwinter cruise. I would continue with, "Are you kidding me? Last time I checked, we're in school. This is going to crush your grade. Ask your parents if there is any other way." *I have never seen a parent change their mind because I made the request.*

So here comes Teacher B's tale of the evermore frequent "I got a deal" vacation.

B had a student that was very marginal *and* operating in a very substantial class, College Prep Chemistry. The semester was two-thirds of the way finished, and the kid had a middle D. Teacher B and "Johnny" had conversations around the idea that maybe a C could be accomplished if Johnny worked a bit harder, turned in all of his missing work, and fundamentally cleaned up his act. In fact, the student was pretty excited about the possibility of raising his grade. Then the fateful day came when Johnny informed Teacher B that he would be taking an extended break around Thanksgiving vacation. There's only four weeks to go in the semester, and the family wants to take the kid out of school for six extra days around both ends of the holiday. Now remember, this is College Prep Chemistry, and it is hard to be gone *one* day, much less six.

Well, the teacher and the student had a heart-to-heart talk, and Teacher B told the young lad that it was a bad idea, from the point of getting a quality grade in the class. In fact, the young guy heard that not only is the possibility of getting a C in the class evaporating, but *now it's probably going to be tough to even pass the class.*

Johnny spent some energy reassuring the teacher that he would make up all of the work when he got back. In fact, he did not make up any of the work when he returned, and yes, you guessed correctly, he failed the class. You may think that he had enough time to right the ship with three weeks to go in the semester, but he actually took the typical track of kids in this situation—he got buried, failed the last two exams of the semester, and finished with an average of barely above 50 percent for the semester. He totally tanked.

Why? I guess it was because Mom and Dad needed to save a little bit of money on the family vacation. Was this whole fiasco worth it? It sure wasn't worth it to Teacher B. He values the education process and passes that along to his students.

Here's an interesting set of similar stories that occurred in the spring of 2006. The first is about a senior girl in one of my Chemistry classes that was on her second shot at the course because she failed it as junior. In fact, she had two different teachers for the course, and the result was the same. The spring promised a new attempt to finish a class that she felt she needed and, in fact, could do very well in. Things began on a pretty solid note with assignments coming in on schedule, and Betty performed well on exams. Then she disappeared for eight days.

I called home after day five, and got Mom on the phone. Basically, I expressed concern and said, "Sup?" The phone receiver bristled with a five-minute explanation as to the fact that Betty couldn't be there the previous week due to continued immaturity and difficulty in "growing up." I listened patiently and told Mom to have her come in and see me the next day. Betty showed up two days later and informed me that she had been in Cancun, Mexico, during the previous week. My brow furrowed as I said, "Cancun?" It seems that Mom forgot to tell me that the family had a standing timeshare week, and that it had not fallen on our school's vacation schedule this year. Wow! "We had a great week, and I am sorry you won't graduate." Did these parents even know what they were doing?

On a more positive note, here's the opposite concept on vacation patterns. What a great story from our math department. In short, a family was preparing to take a trip to Sweden during the fall of 2005. They had a ninth grade son, and he was told to get his work ahead of time so that he wouldn't get the academic drill when he returned. On the Monday he was supposed to start his trip, young Wendall instead showed up in class. He told the entire class that his parents pulled him from the "uber" trip because he had not done the work ahead of time. Instead, he was going to spend a really cool ten days living with his grandma and going to school. *These are starkly different attitudes in parenting.*

Where do you think you would reside in the spectrum?

## Teacher C and "You Just Don't Do This as a Parent"

I've seen a lot of borderline bizarre things from parents, kids, and even teachers over the course of a thirty-three-year career. I think this next story takes the ultimate prize in the "no way" category. The first time I heard it, I almost choked on my lunch because I thought it was a prank—and a really good one at that. When Teacher C told me it was a true story, I was astonished.

This happened in the spring of 2003 to one of our science teachers while he was teaching at another high school in our district. I would say the demographics of this other high school are pretty similar to where we teach. It's a little bit newer building, but the kids seem to be pretty similar. The disease has apparently spread.

Teacher C was teaching sophomores in a biology class and as we all know, sophomores can be a bit goofy. Two of his students were really good friends and both happened to be females. Close friends, for sure, but on this day, only one of them was in class (call her student A). Class began after the teacher took roll, and soon thereafter he noticed that student A had her cell phone out on the desk. This is a real no-no. Everybody in the class knows that Teacher C may snap if that thing goes off. Within a few minutes, the teacher noticed that A was sending a text message. He slipped around to the back of her desk and caught her in the act when he said, "Who have you been text messaging?" She was pretty flustered and then eventually admitted that she has been communicating with her absent best buddy, student B. Ouch!

Now the toaster was starting to warm up. The teacher continued by asking student A, "So where is B?" A's the cover queen and said, "Oh, she's sick today." I guess that implies that she was at home. Well the incoming text message from B painted a different picture when it arrived with the teacher standing there, and said, "Why don't you come to see me?" He looked at A and said, "What? Come and see me?" A was now in that toaster and starting to smoke, so she gave up the truth. "Well … the truth is that B is actually here at school." Teacher A was confused beyond belief.

Remember now that these were sophomores. He then directed student A to text back with the question about her buddy's whereabouts in the building. The answer that comes back was that she is in her mother's room. That's where it starts to get good—student B's mother is a fellow Biology teacher at this high school and a working colleague of Teacher A. The kid—the absent one—had a paper due in class that day and didn't have it done. So rather than go to class, she hid out in her mother's room for the period. Now, you may be thinking that Mom couldn't have known all of this was going on. Oh, she did! *And she was part of the plot.*

I think the frosting on the cake was found in this fact: Mom knew what was going on and had called the attendance office to excuse her daughter's absence so the work would not be counted late. When Teacher C confronted *his colleague* (Mom) about the whole incident, she dropped a litany of lame excuses in an attempt to minimize the issue. She thought it was "No big deal."

I guess that's the whole point of this book in a capsule. Hey, it *is* a big deal! You are raising your child to respect what? Many times this kind of bogus cover is applied by parents, and the kids think, "It's no big deal."

This parent just sacrificed her working trust with a colleague, blew her kid's academic reputation out of the water, and made it to the mountaintop of bad parenting with one quick decision. What was she thinking? What are all of us parents thinking?

# Student Views and
# Model Families

Is this whole "softness" thing that big of a deal? I am clearly of that mindset, and I am about to share that view from other perspectives. I am going to "release" the author's reins a bit in this chapter and call on some direct contributions from some of our students.

The final part of this chapter involves some of the finest examples I've seen in parenting. Here come the students. I asked four of my 2005–2006 students to contribute to the writing of this book. Three of the four have been extremely successful, and one student has, by their own admission, been a big-time underachiever. It will be interesting to see if you can identify these kids from their writings. These are unedited pieces, so the styles are highly variable. So here's how they see the issue from their very personal points of view. Again, these are unedited pieces. I hope they can write well enough.

## Jake J—Senior Spring 2006

First off, before I tell you about my past and observational experiences, I would like give you a little bit of a background about me. I am a graduate of Pomona High School. I had worked hard for everything that I had been given. I was involved in Honors and AP courses since my first year of high school. I wasn't in the advanced courses necessarily because I was that much smarter than the rest of my class, but because I worked that much harder to get what I wanted and because I always respect a good challenge.

I noticed myself struggling through the classes' workloads and meeting expectations at first, but I eventually worked my way to a successful completion of all of my courses. Also in my high school career, I had attempted to play basketball all four years but only succeeded during two of the four. Sophomore year I was cut, and Senior year I had broken my wrist at a preseason practice which caused me to sit out for sixteen weeks.

My Freshman year with the Pomona basketball team was when I had the opportunity to meet Mr. Smiley. His workouts were among the most tiring and productive workout programs that I have ever been involved in. I was constantly pushed to work for things that I had wanted in his program, and after the work, there was always some type of reward.

Whether it is making the team, earning playing time, or only gaining the coaches' respect, there was always a reward. His program was probably the best fit for my personality, and it was hard for me to hear that he was retiring as a basketball coach after only my freshman year because I had seen a future in his program. Even though the coaching of Mr. Smiley had ended earlier than I had hoped, he still helped teach me to never give up and that there was always a reward for hard work. Coach Smiley was the first person in the world, outside of my family, to prove to me that there was always a pay-off for strong efforts. As of today, if I want something, I will get it. If I have my efforts maximized I can get anything that I want.

I was brought up to work for everything that I wanted in my life. Even as a very young child, I was taught that if I had helped my parents with simple household chores I would have earned that Batman action figure. I think because of the fact that my parents had attempted to show me responsibility early, it caused me to always work to my full potential, or pretty close to it. I remember distinctly when I was about three years old, I had helped my parents put up Christmas decorations for hours. My parents were impressed with my attention span for my age. A couple days later when I went to the store with my father, I saw the coolest racecar track that I had ever seen. When I asked my dad if I could get it, he responded, "Son, you'll have to earn it first."

"What's that?" I asked puzzled.

"Earning something is when you do a certain amount of work, or helping someone to the point where you can get something that you want."

"Oh," I said. "I helped you with the Christmas stuff."

"Well … uh … er … yeah you did." He said.

"So can I get it?" I asked.

That is when he used the excuse that he didn't have enough money on him to pay for it, and he told me that I could get it next time I come to the store with my mom. I was ok with that. I was actually pretty excited about learning the fact that I could get anything that I wanted by just working for it.

I had come up through both elementary school and Junior High School without actually noticing my hunger for challenge and success. When I was in fourth grade, I was one of two kids in my class that were placed in a gifted and talented program. It was me, and this nerdy math-wiz type of kid. The program was called OZ. I was afraid at first because back then a program with a name like that would be a program for retarded kids or something. I was excited when I found out it was a class for the advanced kids. I had no idea why I had been chosen, so I guess I had just decided that the only possible explanation was that I was a genius. My head swelled for the few years that I was in that program, but it was worth it.

Towards the end of my eighth grade year was when I had really started to notice the difference between my peers and me. I actually remember the exact moment. One of the counselors from Pomona High School had come by to tell us about registration and options that were available. He came to our science class and gave out all the general necessary paperwork for registration. He then asked if anybody was interested in the Honors English program. Surprisingly, out of everyone in my science class, I was the only student to raise my hand. I didn't quite understand why. We were all in the same class, with the same teacher, and many of us had close to the same grades. I then started to wonder if I had heard everything that the counselor had said, and I had started to second guess my decision. After speaking with my parents and reading over the paperwork, I had decided that I should at least attend the testing trial and see whether or not the class was for me. I attended the session and I had noticed that I was about one of three males in my testing room, whereas there were over 100 applicants.

When I had realized that the honors courses were more challenging, I saw that they scare away the softies. Even though there were 30–40 students who didn't make it in the class, I must give those students credit because they at least put out an effort to accept a challenge. Out of about 75 total students accepted, I was one of six males. I had decided to proceed into the program and I continued through it throughout my entire high school career. I went into the program with a sixth grade reading level.

I struggled throughout my freshman, sophomore, and junior years because I had terrible reading comprehension and it took me relatively 3 times as much time to read a section than my peers of my honors classes. I still worked, and received nothing less than a B until second semester of my Junior year. That was the first year which I was enrolled in a college level course, which was AP English and Literature. I had gotten my first C in a program that I had struggled through for three years prior.

I was labeled by my friends as an "over-achiever." That, personally, made me laugh. It actually felt really good to be labeled as an over-achiever, while the really smart kids were labeling me as a "slacker." I was the overachiever because I would often turn down outings with friends to do my homework. I was the slacker because it took me such a great effort to progress through the courses. I laughed at both sides and continued exactly how I had in the past.

Senior year I had chemistry with Mr. Smiley. He was among the most motivational and best teachers that I have ever had a class with, plus he is one of the funniest guys I know. Mr. Smiley had definitely brought the softness of today's youth, even on the first day. I remember that he had told us that "we are becoming snake people" because of the evolution of hello greetings that kids use when they see their friends in the hall.

He said that when he was in high school, friends would say "hey man, how are you doing?" Then it evolved to "what's up?" Now people say only "sup." I laughed when Mr. Smiley had said that "pretty soon we will just be saying 'sssss.'"

My reaction to this demonstration was that it was initially funny. As I look at it now, he is right, just a greeting in the hall has gotten lazier, as is much of today's youth.

I started to look at kids with a new view. Some kids at school had very expensive cars, whereas they didn't have to pay a dime for it. I started to realize how hard life is going to be for them. If their parents had given everything to them their entire life, they won't know how to work for things when needed. I drive a 1978 Monte Carlo, I paid for every penny…one dollar. The car ran, and it had a pretty cool shape, that was all that I was concerned about for my first car. I did put an expensive CD player in it, because I too am a little soft.

Another thing that I had started to look at differently was the type of kids that would always whine about being tired because they were up so early for school. That one I did not understand because if they get so tired, then why don't these kids go to bed earlier? I would get up at five every morning to watch Sports Center before school, and to finish up any unfinished homework. Some days it was tough, but it was easier for me than other kids to do that because I would go to sleep between 9:30 and 10:00 every night. I was still working with 7 and 8 hours of sleep.

Lastly, I must say that I have been noticing the softness more and more. I'm not quite sure if it is that they are getting softer, or I'm just paying close enough attention. I love it when seniors and juniors in high school have a problem with a teacher, and they have their parents call. That is probably one of the funniest and most entertaining areas of softness. It's not that tough to confront a teacher, but it's not that easy either. Depending on the teacher of course, it can sometimes take a lot of courage to start an argument with one. That is when the softies have the parents deal with the issue.

At this point it is hard to tell how rapidly the softness of American kids is growing, but I do know that it is a growing problem; I will probably watch things from this perspective for the rest of my college and work careers. I will get to see how it evolves and how soft kids turn into soft people. I do know however how I will raise my children, and it will not be soft at all. My house is going to be like a boot camp, and its going to get ugly if they get soft. As for me, I want to thank Mr. Smiley and my parents for producing an anti-soft kid, who is close to the last of a dying breed.

## Hannah L.—Sophomore Spring 2006

Teddy bears, feathers, pillows, kittens, puppies, and rabbits. All of these objects, whether inanimate or living, are soft to the *touch*. It has been observed in society that in addition to objects and organisms *feeling* soft, some humans are *acting* soft. We as individuals can be sensitive creatures, but we also have the natural instinct to be the hunters—to be tough.

According to Webster's Dictionary, the definition of soft has a sundry of meanings. Some of the definitions are as follows: not strong or robust, delicate, incapable of great endurance or exertion; easily influenced or swayed; foolish. While each individual's definition of soft may vary, being called "soft" while in Mr. Smiley's chemistry class was never a compliment.

While taking chemistry with Mr. Smiley as a sophomore in high school, I learned that the word "soft" has more than one meaning. I had always thought of the word as an adjective to describe the feel of objects. I had never considered uttering a person's name with "soft" in the same sentence until I set foot in the chemistry classroom. That year is when my outlook on people's actions changed.

Sitting in the classroom on the first day of school with twenty-five juniors and seniors felt natural to me. After all, it was my second year of high school, and I had been in this situation before because I had previously taken classes with upperclassmen. These upperclassmen seemed to be more interested in surveying the appearances of their peers than paying attention to our syllabus. They socialized, passed notes, and looked bored while I sat bright-eyed and bushy-tailed in the front of the classroom looking forward to another great year of school.

During that fifty-minute class period, I found myself doing push-ups on the linoleum because Mr. Smiley said that we were too soft. If we were going to survive the semester, we were going to have to toughen up, and it was his belief that giving twenty push-ups every now and then would help our endurance.

Being one of two sophomores in the class, I was an easy target for teasing. It is surprising, though, that the instigator in this situation was my teacher. Mr. Smiley seemed to have this tradition of naming his sophomores "Rookie" instead of calling them by name. And with this announcement on the first day of school at my new school, I became known as "The Rookie."

As the semester intensified, I intensified as well. With Mr. Smiley perpetually on my case because of my age, I had fuel to prove him wrong. I landed on his "top dog" list after every major quiz throughout the school year. I answered tough questions in class while my peers sat staring at the board in wonder. I completed every assignment with punctuality, and I went about my labs with enthusiasm.

As I began gaining Mr. Smiley's respect, I began gaining the respect of my classmates as well. At the beginning of the year, my classmates were a very tough crowd to befriend because: 1) I was a rookie, 2) I was the new kid at school, 3) I had transferred from one of the rival schools, and 4) I intimidated a lot of my peers with my intelligence.

At first, no one wanted to admit that I was doing just as well, or better, than the upper classmen. But as time progressed, and they saw that I would be able to teach them things, they became friendlier. They even started acknowledging me in the hall with a quick wave or a "Hi, Rookie."

For the first semester, more than one half of my class did not know my actual name. They only knew that I was the smart sophomore answering questions in class. As the climate became friendlier, I began talking more to my classmates.

On two or three days a week, we would have a warm-up to give our brains a jump-start. These warm-ups were fondly known as deviant thinker questions, or "DTQs." Like everyone else, I missed a few every now and then. On one particular, crisp fall day, we had a DTQ involving a tree and leaves. One of the athletes that sat near me asked me in all seriousness how to spell "rake." I have to admit, I figured that by the time you're in eleventh grade, you should know how to spell a basic four letter word. So instead of helping him, I laughed. After hearing our little conversation, Mr. Smiley snapped and ordered me to give ten push-ups for teasing this guy. And because I had learned by October that I was not soft, I quickly completed my task.

The joking, the teasing, and the push-ups continued throughout the semester. I conquered all of Mr. Smiley's tasks, proving that I was definitely not soft. In fact, I finished the semester with a high A. This grade also happened to be one of the highest out of any of Mr. Smiley's students.

In January, I once again set foot in Mr. Smiley's class for another fun-filled semester of chemistry, DTQs, and teasing. However, for my second semester, I had Mr. Smiley for first period, and as everyone who has had Mr. Smiley knows, being late to class is one of the worst sins.

At first, the whole class had to give push-ups if one person was late because Mr. Smiley believed that the whole class should repent for the tardy student's sins. As the semester wore on, and it was the same group of people that were always tardy, we abandoned the theory of repenting. After all, it wasn't the majority of us that were soft; it was the five teenagers that could not drag themselves out of bed.

Because of all of my hard work the previous semester, Mr. Smiley no longer thought that I was soft. And I was still a rookie, but my name was upgraded to the "Legendary Rookie," and sometimes the "Super Rookie."

Throughout both semesters, in addition to learning about the fascinating world of chemistry, I learned a new definition of soft. The students that were soft were always the ones that were tardy, sleepy, missed review sessions because it was too early, forgot about homework, and did poorly on quizzes because they didn't have a few extra minutes to study.

One of the culminating events of the second semester was our extra credit session at Denny's for an early morning breakfast and a chemistry lesson. In order to attend, students couldn't have any blanks in the grade book, and they had to atone for three or more tardies by cleaning desks or mopping the science classrooms. The time that we met was the perfect time between night and morning: 3:37 am. After all of the requirements were met, we had the option to go, if we wanted. But the policy for that morning was that we had to be early. We couldn't be any later than 3:37 because Mr. Smiley would lock the doors and we would laugh and wave and persuade the sleepy head to go home and back to bed.

Needless to say, I was there, proving that I was a tough rookie. While other kids were disoriented and trying to secretly snooze in the booth, I was once again bright eyed and bushy tailed. We were given a worksheet that was partially review and partially new material. With the cooperation of the others sitting at my table, we were the first group to finish the entire worksheet correctly.

As it is easy to imagine, there were some very tired puppies in class that day. But I, a studious sophomore that loved chemistry, was one of the only students that was coherent the entire day. I even would have done it again if asked.

Seeing Mr. Smiley skeptical on one hot day in August when I first entered his classroom only added fuel to my already intense fire. At first he didn't believe that I could succeed. Under his tough love, though, I blossomed and flourished. While taking chemistry and seven other challenging, intellectual courses, I maintained my 4.0 gpa. I earned a spot on the "top dog" list after every major quizz that we took in class. I worked my way from the ground up to a very high "A" both semesters. I was privileged enough to be selected onto the school chemistry team for the state competition, where I took third place with my partner in the element identification event, and where our team as a whole took first place overall. And finally, I earned a silver test tube for having the most correct answers in our pre-examination competitions.

While all of these awards are great, the highlight of my year was earning the respect of Mr. Smiley. With his guidance, I came to realize that science is my forte, and I should stick with it. I also came to realize that when I have a doubter or a skeptic trying to bring me down, all I have to do is show who I really am in order to prove them wrong. I am a fighter who is always willing to take a challenge.

It seems that to Mr. Smiley, everyone is soft. But after spending a year in his classroom, I have learned that he is just provoking us to bring out our best. Holding study sessions at 6 am was preparing us for the massive amount of studying and the berserk hours that we will maintain while in college. Having us do push-ups in class taught us discipline, self-respect, and control. Giving us reading quizzes over material that he didn't go over was preparation for college and careers. And giving me a hard time was preparing me for any uphill battles that I will have to fight in the future.

While I have always known that teddy bears, feather, pillows, kittens, puppies, and rabbits are soft, I have learned that people are soft. The people that have excuses to get out of any job or chore are soft. The people that value sleep more than life itself are soft. The people that are late habitually are soft. The people that forget to turn in assignments or complete important tasks are soft. At the beginning of tenth grade, I was a bit of a softie. By the end of tenth grade, I was a tough, smart young woman, ready to take on whatever obstacle or battle that life decides to throw in my way.

## Grant B.—Senior Spring 2006

I wouldn't say I'm soft, but I often had my priorities out of order. And I got bored, very quickly. All that mixed together with a touch of laziness (okay, maybe more than a touch) and you get a snapshot of my high school career—good intentions but never really measuring up to what I knew I could do.

Not to say that I didn't try. I gave it my best shot, but things just kept coming up. It's almost as if the powers that be, just to test my resolve, would throw crisis after crisis at me to see if I still stood in the aftermath.

My mother's mantra to me was "You have such potential—why aren't you using it?" I heard it day after day, week after week. Every time the phone rang and the auto caller from school said I had missed a day or was failing a class, my mom would give me that look that crushed my heart more than any grounding or punishment could ever do—it was the look of sheer disappointment.

And then there was the boredom. If there are only AP classes and normal classes—I fit somewhere in the middle: challenging concepts but little homework. Unfortunately, classes don't work that way; it's either one extreme or the other. And, of course, I chose the easy way out. It's a great way to catch up on sleep, but not very conducive to learning anything.

I knew the material, and the teacher always taught at

a few levels below me, so it got boring quickly. I refuse to do busy work because it's all repetitive and a waste of my time and I refused to go to class because it's nothing new.

Then I got that surprise F on my report and wondered, "Why, if I knew it all, did I fail?"

And then, if all that wasn't enough, there is my incredible laziness. Many of my teachers can attest to the fact that I am one of those students who will wait until the very last minute to do something I don't want to do. If I am passionate about it, it will get done quickly, but those projects were very few and far between.

It's a question I've been trying to answer since the end of my sophomore year. Why, if I am so smart or have "such potential" am I not in the top of my class with a 4.0 GPA like everyone said I should have?

I could blame it on circumstance. Sure, the long lasting depression I went through and the divorce that separated my parents would pass as wonderful excuses. And maybe saying that I work three nights a week just to pay my bills would get some sympathy. It follows that homework is just not something I can afford to spend my precious time on.

But to my credit, I skipped on the sob stories with my teachers. I just swallowed what I was handed, and shut-up. Unfortunately, this caused my teachers to think that I was involved in drugs or something and they quit caring. Some stayed with me, but most just gave me the grade I earned and left it at that, figuring I was far too lost to be saved from my own downfall.

If you put all those together, I guess you'll get the picture that I had the right stuff to succeed but I just didn't take the opportunity I was afforded.

I won't sit here and tell you that fate dealt me a bum hand and that my misfortune was the stuff of some sick God's joke on me. I accept every bit of responsibility in what happened to me, and I guess that's the problem that I see with some people—they just don't take responsibility for why they are where they are, or they lie and cheat their way to a false accomplishment.

Maybe I am being hard on myself, or on others—but when day after day you see the same girl cheat on her tests and homework, and get a better grade than you because you refuse to compromise your honor for a few points—and then you get the rap of being the lazy guy, you start to lose faith in things.

I was raised in a good home. I may not be a phenomenal child, but I have two parents whom I love to death and who raised me as best they could. They taught me to be honest, to never cheat and to work for what I earn. I was rarely handed something I didn't earn, and I've held a job since it was legal to do so.

But maybe that girl didn't get the discipline I've gotten. Maybe, she was handed things she never earned and has got the idea in her head that as long as she doesn't get caught that it's alright.

I guess it's alright—I mean, how much is one's integrity worth to you? An 'A' on a major test? A couple hundred dollars?

Personally, I would rather earn what I deserve, even if that is an F and a ticket to summer school.

It's a weird situation I am in, I have the discipline to take what I earn, and not accept what I don't—and yet I can't seem to sit down and do my homework.

Maybe you need to care also—care about the work and the grade. I can sit down and hammer out a novel if I care enough, but give me some redundant busy work, and nothing in the world can make me do it.

Not even my diploma, apparently.

Where I am right now in life, is a result of my own actions and reactions to the things that have happened to me. Sure, I didn't get the ideal shot at Valedictorian that I would have like, but I made it.

Maybe the problem with our youth (my peers) and the generations to follow is a lack of responsibility we seem to have for our actions. The major prevailing thought with my peers is that the ends justify the means, which basically says that cheating, lying, stealing, and whatever you do to get out successfully and get to a good college is fine.

I should have worked harder, and done what I was capable of doing, but I did what I felt was necessary and I don't have any regrets. At least I know I earned what I got, and that in college, I have a brand new chance to actually apply myself at something I actually care about.

## Andrew S.—Senior Spring 2006

When time is undersized and there are a plethora of reasons for quitting, it is imperative to buckle down and do everything possible to succeed. Everywhere I look there is hard work to be done. A lot of people are triumphant in their efforts, but not everyone uses the same approach to get there. Certain people are very strong willed and push themselves based solely on desire, while others constantly have to be set in motion by those around them in order to do well. It is important to set goals for that are difficult but reachable.

If goals are not set, it may be difficult to have the mindset to attain a particular level and even harder to know if the level reached could have been surpassed. On the other hand, if the set goals are unreachable and end up unfulfilled, it can be easy to become frustrated and disappointed. Both of these have negative effects, thus it is important to have reasonable aspirations.

A lot of young teenagers think it is "not cool" to do well in school, and if he or she does well it might make them look "different." Something that works for me is to really try and be an individual. Personal experience has shown me that being a teenager is the time when everyone tries to figure out who they are and what they are going to be. I have noticed that a lot of adolescents try to be too much like their peers in this stage of life. I have found it is really important to be my own person, set my own goals, set my own limitations, find what I like and go for it.

I know this saying is pounded into the turf, but it really is important not to give into peer pressure. If I find myself spending countless hours on homework each night and my friends are spending half the time, it should not been seen as a negative. It is important that everyone spends the amount of time fit to them and not the quantity of time it takes other people to get things done. Even though it may take longer, it is really important not to copy another student's work; I know it is not going to expand my knowledge. Instead, I ask someone who knows the material to guide me in the right direction.

I mentioned earlier that some individuals are more self-motivated than others, but it does help to have someone there to supply a nudge in the right direction. For me, my parents have always been there to keep me on track. From grade school to present day, I have constantly been expected to be an "A" student, with an occasional "B" being acceptable.

When I was younger, my mother and my father would study with me, get me to school on time, help me with homework and make sure I was always doing it properly. Once high school hit, the assignments became tougher, I was able to drive myself to school, and wanted to become a lot more independent in my studies. At this point, my parents were not able to help me as much and took a step back in order for me to formulate my own responsibility. Instead of constantly hassling me about school, an occasional, "How is everything in school going?" would come about.

This has been really helpful for me, knowing that my parents still care, but are willing to accept the fact that I am growing up. A laid back attitude has been the approach for the last few years, but when grades are handed out, my parents are all business. If my grades are up to standard everything is fine, but if I come home with anything less than satisfactory grades (which, fortunately, is a rarity) I will hear about it.

I place my parents in high regard because the way they have raised me has worked for me just as much as it has for them. They could not have done much more to support me. However, others may need more attention, or a watchful eye that lasts well beyond the first year of high school. If this were the case for me, it would have been effective for my parents to pester me until I grew enough to thrive on my own. Fortunately, the approach my parents have taken has done wonders, not only in the classroom, but with the rest of my life as well.

Knowing that I have the ability to perform is one thing, but making sure I actually do well is another. It is really easy to say "I can't do it" or "What's the point?" It is also common to occupy time with enjoyable activities, rather than those that actually take discipline. I have been fortunate that I find joy in being disciplined, which is not the case for a lot of people my age. Of course I feel like giving up once in a while, but deep down I know that it is going to feel so high quality to do the right thing. Whether it is staying up late to finish an English paper, getting up at four in the morning to take my sister to the airport, or putting in that extra hour a night practicing for baseball, I feel excellent about it once it is done, knowing I went about it the right way.

There have been many times when I put a half-assed effort into something and felt terrible about it for days. After enough of those, I was able to realize that not wanting to feel terrible is enough to make me put forth a full-fledged effort. Obtaining self discipline and the desire to feel proud of myself has helped me stay on top of things, and kept me away from quitting.

There are often instances where I find myself on the border between one thing and another. I cannot even remember how many times I have had a high "B" and known I had to go for it, or had a low "A" and recognized that I could not let it get away. Since this happens to me frequently, I know that I have to push myself even harder than usual. It generally means a lot more studying, additional practice on homework, and asking loads of questions. If I do not put in that extra amount of effort, it will be tough to accept the outcome, knowing it is not what I wanted.

School is a lot of fun, especially when the hard work results in a high reward. It is not easy, but it can be less stressful if proper actions are taken. I make an effort toward getting a lot of sleep each night because it makes learning easier and more enjoyable. I also make a strong attempt to get an early jump on my homework each day so that I have free time in the evenings and more time for sleep. If I do not understand something I ask someone who might know the answer or, better yet, go to school early and ask the teacher for assistance. Being to class on time is essential because I do not miss anything and I cannot be punished for being tardy. These responsibilities are painless to take care of and will aid me in my accomplishments.

I cannot emphasize enough how important it is not to use other people as a crutch. If I do not attempt things for myself, it is going to be a rude awakening in the future. I have to put in that extra effort, learn from mistakes, and take pride in my work. I have been witness to people growing up around me and I know there is no limitation to what a person can do in a lifetime.

## Summarizing the Students

Is it apparent that kids have a grip on the issue? It doesn't seem to matter if the student has had personal success in education or only limited success. You can't fool them. They know what they are and more importantly, what they want to become. They want that success and along with it, the toughness it takes to get there. Mental strength is a very positive quality. How have some parents seemed to be able to "coach" the strength into their kids while others seem to get stuck in the daily quagmire of little battles with the kids? What's the secret of successful parenting?

## Successful Parenting 1980s–2000s

I'm going to shift gears again and give you examples of two families that I've seen do some exquisite parenting. I have had many families provide multiple children to my classes over the years, and there is a bit of a pattern to the family situations. Successful methods work with a wide variety of kids. Here are two family examples that worked their magic really well. The two time periods are about fifteen years apart, but their techniques and courage in parenting will work for eternity. One family is traditional and one is not, but they're both successful.

## The Keck Family

The first example is a traditional two-parent family that produced three of my students from 1980–1987. The Keck family consisted of Tom and Barb Keck and their three children: Todd (class of 1981), Melissa (class of 1984), and Matt (class of 1987). I always admired how the Keck kids conducted their business as high school students. I sought out Dad in the summer of 2006 to talk about the offspring. I had no doubt that they would be quite successful when they left high school; I just didn't know the specifics.

How could I have been so sure that three very different kids would ultimately be independent, self-sufficient, and successful twenty or thirty years later? I knew because the quality of the parenting was so solid. After sitting with Tom Keck for about two hours, I have a lot of specific parenting techniques to share with you. It's a solid system that is based on developing the young kid's ability to take care of him or herself. Here's a little background on each of their children first.

---

My experience with Todd Keck in high school Chemistry was very good. He was the typical bright-eyed suburban kid that had a positive view every day. Did he work to his maximum potential every day? Probably not, but he was pretty good. I thought he was destined for the typical four-year college scene after graduation, and then we had an event occur at Pomona. The army, in a recruiting tactic, flew an Apache helicopter to PHS and landed it on the football field for students to inspect.

Todd Keck was hooked instantly. He enlisted in the army shortly thereafter, even though Dad told him not to do it without talking about it. I was amazed when I heard the story.

I told him at the time that he would find himself to

be one of the smartest guys in the regular army, and they must have felt that way as well, because they sent him to West Point after only one year. Todd subsequently received his degree in mechanical engineering, became an officer, and eventually fought in the 1991 Gulf War. He did well enough to return to Saudi Arabia later as a consultant, and today he is an FBI agent. Papa Tom describes him as "Very clear, very definite, and very confident." I'd call him successful. *He took an indirect path to success.*

---

Melissa was an excellent high school student and very well adjusted socially. She gave the impression of being able to talk to anybody at any time. I think I found the reason why when Dad and I talked recently. Papa Tom is a Ph.D. who worked the rigors of junior high counseling for twenty-seven years. His area of specialty is "communication training," and he felt that Melissa could benefit from a dose of it growing up.

It seems that the daughter came home one day in eighth grade and announced that she wanted to try out for cheerleading. Mom and Dad approved, but there was a caveat. She had to do "communication training" with Dad. This was not a minor commitment. Melissa agreed to the full year of training and subsequently became a cheerleader.

Later in time, she wanted out of the communication training, and Mom and Dad took a unique approach to the request. If she wanted to stop, Melissa had to provide an alternate choice of how she would be spending that time. In short, she had to bring the solution to the table. Her proposal was that she would go out for track and volleyball instead, which worked well with the folks. *She had to solve her own issue. Mom and Dad provided legitimate choices for the kid to make.*

Today, Melissa has completed her sixteenth year as a successful elementary school teacher.

———————

Matt was different to raise than his older brother and sister. Dad indicates that the older kids were pretty compliant, but Matt always wanted to test the edges of what was acceptable. One of the family rules was that young kids had to be in when it got dark. Not a problem for kids number one and number two. Matt wanted to know "What was the definition of dark?" Huh? He indicated one night that he could still see the outline of the mountains, so it couldn't be dark. Wow. He needed a more definite rule. The one that Tom liked was, "You have to be in if the street lights are on." Matt needed that black and white approach.

As a high school student, Matt Keck was very bright, very sociable, and yet didn't always feel like being the ultimate academician. He went to college for one year, didn't return for number two, and eventually became a master plumber. Without any question, he's very successful today. His skills are highly recognized, his responsibilities are immense, and he does well economically. *Matt did not follow the traditional pathway. He found his own.*

———————

I don't think many families devise a formal system of raising their kids, but many times it becomes one nonetheless.

I asked some questions of Tom Keck that fall into the "How did you do it?" category, and here are some pearls of wisdom. *It is very important to remember that this was a traditional two-parent family situation.* The next example is from a one-parent system that also worked very well.

Tom describes the parenting roles like this. He would usually be the one to "go nuts" when some type of problem occurred. Barb was always "real calm." It almost sounds like the good cop/bad cop system. Actually, I would probably say it was more like the "stay balanced" system. Think of the old playground here: it's like a teeter-totter. If one parent is hot, it's probably good for the other to be cool, etc. Probably the best situation is balance—when the two people on the teeter-totter are able to hang in mid-air. You can rise or fall a bit, but it's always good to come back to a balanced location.

Tom and Barb Keck were also at the top of the parenting game for another very big reason. They always sought to engage and communicate regularly with their children. Since there were two parents in this situation, they felt it was important (and I concur) that they present a consistent model for the kids to see on a daily basis.

Tom made a point of telling me that the kids always knew if they told one parent something, the other one would hear about it shortly. That's not to say there wasn't some kind of exception made in the process. But as a general rule, the parents were consistent and yes, somewhat predictable in the kids' eyes. *It wasn't possible to drive a wedge between Mama and Papa Keck.*

*A Big Event:*

In each of the parenting examples, I'm identifying a

big event in the eyes of the family, where one of the kids had a major issue crop up. As a parent, you are at a crossroads of what to do. I like how the Keck's situation turned out through outstanding parenting.

When the youngest child, Matt, was in either fourth or fifth grade, Pops received a call from the oldest son, telling him Matt was in trouble for starting a fire at his elementary school. Tom needs to deal with the problem immediately. How would you react if you received such a call? Would you be open-minded, or would you be ready to defend immediately?

Much happened in the time Dad headed for the principal's office. It had been determined that Matt didn't start the fire. However, young Matthew did find some matches and didn't turn them in, which apparently was the school policy. Additionally, while the four young lads were in the outer room awaiting the principal, they were "passing gas and laughing about it." This was straight from the principal to Dad. Finally, the principal wanted Matt to stay after school for one week as a disciplinary measure for the farting episode. Dad said okay, even though he didn't necessarily agree with it. *Dad supported the school system.*

On the walk home, Matt asked his dad, "Are you mad?" Tom's response was classic. He said, "No, but I'm disappointed that you were farting in the office." Matt then told Tom that nobody was doing that, and in fact, one kid was doing the "arm fart" in a realistic way. Matt laughed, but that was it.

The next Monday saw the first day of detention, and when Dad arrived home, Matt was sitting in the living room waiting for him. "This isn't fair. I didn't do that stuff." After a bit more explanation, it became apparent to Dad that Matt wanted him to call the principal and get the punishment reduced. Tom said no but recommended to Matt that he should make an appointment (on his own) with the principal and then go in and plead his own case. *The kid was going to learn something here!* By Tuesday afternoon, Matt had his meeting and was excused from future detention. *How many of us would go the same route as a parent?*

The Kecks were exceptional parents, but then, we all want to be exceptional. I asked Tom near the end of the interview, "What one quality did you feel your kids had to have developed when they left your influence at age eighteen?"

Tom thought about it for a few minutes while I chased the coffee and then said two words upon my return. "Personal responsibility."

Tom had other great perspectives on parenting:

"If you don't want to deal out discipline because it will affect your relationship with the kid, you already have a crappy relationship."

"A lot of times, kids need to be able to make choices. It helps them develop as an adult."

As a counselor in junior high, he would sometimes hear this from a parent, "Johnny is not doing well because he's bored."

Tom Keck's response, "Boredom is a feeling. What's he going to do about it?"

All of the Keck kids are different. But all of them take care of themselves in very successful ways.

## The Hodapp Family

This is a very different story from the Keck family, and yet I think it represents a lot of households in America today. There is no two-parent structure, yet it functions very much like the traditional family, even though it has one parent in charge on a daily basis. Dee Hodapp and her husband divorced many years ago when the two kids were very young. In essence, Jenna and Nick remember their upbringing as always having been in a single-parent household.

Dee would tell you herself that there were many moments of immense difficulty, and yet she exhibited a toughness and a degree of determination that would mold her kids for their entire lifetimes. I sat with Dee for a two-hour session and learned the chronology of that parental determination. I have had both Jenna and Nick in my class and have seen the benefits of strong parenting. They were very different kids (from each other) in my classes over a three-year period, but they shared the commonality of future success. They had been prepared for it over the past couple of decades.

---

Jenna is twenty-two years old and just recently graduated from college, where she received her degree in speech communications. I first saw her as a senior in high school in one of our advanced Science Seminar classes called Field Geology. Recall that successful completion of this class earns the student three semester hours of credit from the University of Colorado system. It is an extremely difficult class where entrance is granted via a competitive application process. Jenna had no trouble competing.

The basis of the seminar program is to take our top juniors and seniors in our science department and challenge them with classes that have them "doing science" on a daily basis, rather than just taking another text and lecture class. The students have to collect and analyze their own field data, construct their own maps, etc. It's not a class for the faint of heart.

Jenna Hodapp was outstanding in this situation. I'd have to say that her ability to organize her work and be productive was among the very best I have ever seen. Other teachers tell the same story from other classes over time. And yet she was also a very balanced young woman with interests in many areas other than just academics. She was tough, and she was focused. For years I wondered why this was so evident.

When I asked Mom the inevitable question of why Jenna was this way, Dee shed some interesting light on the upbringing. Expectations grew from Mom's own upbringing and affected how she raised her kids. I think that happens to all of us to some degree. By her own account, Dee says she was raised as a farmer's daughter in the 1960s and 1970s,and since she was a girl, the expectation was directed toward an academic career. Dee didn't feel that it was a bad upbringing by any means, but the view was too limited. Consequently, Dee had a line for her daughter, Jenna, that was expressed many times over the nurturing years: "You have to be twenty-five and have a degree in your hand before you even think of getting married." *Expectations and possible life opportunities may have been opened up with this edict.*

Today, Jenna Hodapp is ready to embark on life with many worlds available to her. I know she has the tools to do what she wants in life. Expect her to succeed.

---

I want to ask you readers with more than one kid a significant question: Didn't you think kid number two would be a lot like number one? And then it happened, and they were different in more ways than they were similar. This was true in the Hodapp case as well. As they say in the new school lingo, Nick's a trip.

I actually remember Nick Hodapp's first day in my Chemistry class his junior year in high school. He was the guy with more energy than all of the other kids in class combined. Even though he was semi-electric, he was always respectful and under control. He fit in well, was really comfortable, and I had only known him for about seven minutes. Wow. Would he be like his sister as a student? No. He was different for about ten million reasons. And that was just fine with me.

Mr. Nick Hodapp was one of the absolute social leaders of his class at Pomona. He could have been one of the academic leaders as well. He was a really quick intellect. His junior year was characterized by pretty much underachieving in the academics and maybe doing "just enough to get by." You might have a son or daughter who currently has the same academic goal as Nick did four years ago. Something happened midway through the experience that I found really intriguing. His dad gave Nick a Toyota four-by-four truck to use on a daily basis, and I heard about it the next day in class. He was pumped up, to say the least. The down side was that he wouldn't be driving it for very long.

Now you have to remember that Mom and Dad Hodapp were divorced with two very distinctly different households. I can't say that one was better or worse for the kids; they were just different. Since Nick was living with Dee on a daily basis, he had to follow her rules and expectations in that household, and at this time in life, he wasn't meeting some of them. One of his apparent shortcomings was his current set of grades, and since they were not high enough for Mom, she took away the truck. That was pretty impressive—she took something away that she hadn't even given him. Now for this to work well, her ex-husband, Jeff, probably had to step up and support Dee; and in fact, he did. Nick would get the truck back when his performances warranted it. Nick had given me the whole scoop in class, and as I said, I was watching this one carefully. I knew Nick could resist the discipline train with an iron-like will.

While the resistance to change was there, Nick eventually complied with Mom's determined efforts. I would say it took a couple of months, but his effort levels improved, and because he was a talented guy, his grade rose in Chemistry. His other grades also improved, and he eventually had a very respectable senior year in high school academia. Mom drew a line in the sand and *didn't waver* when it was tough. *I think this is one of the highest forms of parental love.*

I talked earlier in this chapter about the traditional two-parent methods of working together. That can only truly be the case with two parents in the house on a daily basis. If you are a single parent, *you have to be able and willing to do both jobs,* and as Dee Hodapp expressed recently, "It can be really tough." It's tough for sure, but not impossible.

---

*Final Pearls from D.H.*

According to the U.S. Census Bureau, only 67 percent of the children in America had two married parents in the household in 2006. A significant portion of our American families have only one parent residing with the kids on a daily basis. And yet, the Hodapp family represents a great deal of solid parenting. Interestingly enough, Mom noted that she would *enlist the support of the other kid when trying to work with one kid's problem.* I think it's kind of like tag-team wrestling. When two parents are not around, other siblings can help fill that role.

I then asked Dee to give me some other chunks of advice for parents in a similar situation to hers. Here's some of the best pieces of advice I've heard.

> "Be your kid's friend certainly, but be their parent first."
> "Teach kids to earn what they have. We hand way too much to our kids."
> "They need to earn it. That's going to be a survival skill."

# High School Prep: Will Your Kids Be Ready for College?

The public school system in America is a very complex organism. While the daily and hourly courses make up the majority of a student's day, there is a lot more going on than we always understand. I begin this chapter with a discussion in our counseling center with Ms. Karin Blough. She is a very hard-working lady that can analyze a kid's issues very well and usually very quickly. Karin has no trouble telling both students and parents what is on her mind when it comes to helping the students make quality decisions. We talked last September about how she sees today's students and parents.

## A High School Counselor's View

I began the interview with questions about how Karin herself was raised by her own parents who had emigrated from Holland. They were extremely proud to be Americans, even to the point of *not* teaching their own kids the Dutch language. Her mom and dad had high expectations for their kids, and with regard to how Karin dealt with her teachers and classes, she said, "I never would have thought about coming home and saying, 'Could you call my teacher about…' I think my dad would have been like, 'Suck it up.'" Now I know not everyone wants to take that approach, but Karin indicates that it worked for her family.

If I could oversimplify Karin Blough's daily job, it would be that she helps kids grow up and eventually graduate on time. One of today's impediments to that seems to be how both students and parents approach the personal responsibility issue. "Some kids charm their way at the last minute to get a grade." Maybe you've seen your kid scramble like a rat at the end of a grading period, or maybe you have even helped them do it.

*Excuse me, is there any extra credit Sally could do to raise her grade?* Karin contends that teachers are hurting the kid in the long run when this is allowed to happen. The technique can fail miserably when the student is a senior and people are onto the regular pattern of behavior. Sally doesn't always graduate.

I admittedly asked Karin to give me her most amazing story of parent deviance, and she had a beauty. The fall of 2005 saw a freshman arrive in her office with an unusual story. The semester was already eight or nine weeks old when he arrived, and the parents indicated that he had been ill out of the country for some time. That would explain why he was home-schooled, and there were no records of his attending another school for the past nine weeks.

Ms. Blough went to work for this kid and his parents. She worked with his teachers and sought to have him tested to try to get some credit, even though he had missed a major piece of time. Additionally, she put her professional creditability and reputation on the line when she tried to help him. Then she received a phone call from another high school in the area with a disturbing question. How had our high school enrolled this kid without the normal paperwork? As Karin tried to explain the "out of the country, major illness" issue, the caller interrupted to inform her that "Billy" had in fact attended their school and had been suspended for attendance issues. It seems that the parents were not giving our counseling department the truth. *Once again, what do we teach as parents when we do not hold our kids accountable? When we lie, we teach lying.*

Karin reacted in a fair but definite way. She had every teacher restart the kid at an F level, and Billy had to dig his way out of a very deep cellar. Guess what happened. He dug his way out and passed his courses. Ms. Blough called the parents in to confront them on their lies, and *they* would not let their son attend the conference because it was "their fault." A number of teachers questioned whether or not all of Billy's work was his own *or* did Mom do a lot of it for him? In short, this thing was a real mess. I go back to what Karin Blough's dad would have said in an attempt to help his daughter: "Suck it up." Parents today are really struggling with this line and attitude about parenting. Surely this changes as the kids grow older and get ready to leave for college. You remember what "going to college" is supposed to mean. The young lad or lass has a chance to further their education and also mature in an environment that traditionally has worked for countless numbers of students over the years. This has been deep tradition that has been sought and followed by many families for what seems to be eons. Are today's students ready for college? *More importantly, perhaps, are your kids ready?*

## A Consultant to Help the Transition

Hal Kuczwara is a training consultant that has taught both at the high school and college levels. His company works with a number of high schools in Colorado and seeks to help students prepare for a number of adventures in life, including going to college. A number of his activities involve team-building experiences that help to improve individual self-confidence levels. Hal has taught a freshman seminar course at the University of Colorado for seven years, and one of his standard experiences is to take the students to the ropes course. This involves some elevated experiences where the student questions his or her personal well-being. Hal wants the kid to question whether or not they are safe on the high altitude ropes and what resources do they have at their disposal to "get safe." When I asked Hal why he felt it was important to take eighteen-year-olds through the experience, he said, "The statistics show that 50 percent of all college freshmen drop out. They drop out because they talk themselves out of it. They drop out because of lack of confidence. They drop out because they haven't made connections." Do you question the 50 percent statement as being too high? Let's say it is even 40 percent or 30 percent. *All* of those numbers are too high. *For some reason, our young men and women are not ready for the experience.*

Let's talk about the concept of making connections. Hal talks about another exercise he has used in class with his freshmen. Try this one yourself and see how you approach the task. Stretch a rubber band across the back of your hand with one connection on your little finger and the other across the thumb. Even without the prop, you can envision what this looks like. Now Mr. K tells the student to get the band off his hand without using his other hand, rubbing it on his clothes or the table, etc. The time limit is five seconds. Very few kids are successful with this, but occasionally one seems to have the gift. If they succeed, Hal tells them they must now achieve the feat in less than one second. Are you kidding me? Nobody seems to be able to do it unless they mentally walk around the obstacle. Ask someone to help you! It's the only way to solve the problem.

Hal makes a really critical connection to college success when he says, "A lot of failure in college is about *not* identifying the resources. Nobody should fail college. There are so many resources to help a student succeed. It's a cultural issue for us. I think we don't like to ask for help."

## A College Professor That's Seen the Change

I'm hopeful you will notice that I'm working on a progression here. I've started with the high school teachers and counselors, gone to a college instructor in the area of student transitions to college life, and now I'm ready to give you the view from way up there. Dr. Bob Green, Ed.D., is the interim director of the Eugene T. Moore School of Education at Clemson University. Dr. Green normally is an alumni distinguished professor of education at Clemson, and he has taught both undergraduate and graduate courses in the history and culture of education in America for over twenty years. He has seen a lot of students in those years and has noticed some subtle changes in the kids. He talked with me in December of 2006 and shared some really pertinent experiences. I began the discussion by questioning a new phenomenon that I had heard about from Hal Kuczwara at the University of Colorado.

> Tim Smiley: "Have you seen students go to visit their professors during office hours with either their mom or dad in tow?"
>
> Bob Green: "Oh yeah.'"

I need to sit down for a minute. I'm a product of the seventies, as is Dr. Green, and we both agreed that this kind of thing just did *not* happen back in the day. It is definitely a recent turn of events, and I think a hideous one. Why would anyone feel the need to babysit their offspring with the college professor at age twenty-something? Bob

Green has the two-word answer that he admittedly did not coin. *Helicopter parents.*

I said I needed specific, legitimate, and true examples of this for my readers, and he pulled a few examples from the Clemson archives and shared them with both you and me. Read and be amazed. If you think these could be legitimate examples of parenting, call me, and I will help you find some professional help.

### Example 1

Dr. Green had an interesting talk with a daughter/mother team a few years ago when the young woman was considering attending Clemson as a freshman for the next year. Bob noticed how quiet the kid was, and it seemed like the mother was responding for the team every time. It got to be time for the professor to see whether or not the young lady was mute, so he said directly to the mom, "Let's hear what Leslie's thinking."

*Mom answered the question, even though she was politely told not to do so.*

What drives this kind of behavior? The mother continued to dominate the conversation, much like a Caterpillar D-9 bulldozer dominates dirt.

### Example 2

Clemson University's education program has a set of block courses that must be successfully completed prior to any student going on to student teach in the system. It is a prerequisite for all candidates. Dr. Green talked about a young candidate that received a low grade on a single paper in one of those courses. As a result, the student quit coming to class. (This is exactly the lack of toughness I'm talking about.) Many professors would not worry about the issue and just issue the F at the end of the semester, but this particular professor tried to contact the student by e-mail. The professor got no response, and the student failed.

Since this was a fall semester course, young Wilma wouldn't be able to student teach in the spring, as was the original plan. She let the department know she wanted to student teach in the spring anyway and was denied. End of issue, right? Not with the parents. So how did they respond?

The parents called the department chair *at home on Christmas Day* to plead their case.

Nice touch.


## Example 3

When a young woman or young man begins a career in the working world, parent influence with the new boss is long over. Can I get everyone to agree to that? I mean, what if I call my son Matt's boss and try to explain his sore throat or his not getting a report done on time? No way is that boss going to listen to me.

That's not the real world.

Matt's issue is Matt's. Wilma's issue is Wilma's. And so on., etc.

A twenty-something Clemson student teacher is in the first semester of the experience where a lot of classroom observation takes place. Daily work is done to get the candidate ready to independently take over all of the cooperating teacher's classes in the future. Normally in their system, the candidate continues on with the cooperating teacher to do the formal student teaching, but this time the cooperating teacher declined to have the student teacher back. Why? Had something happened between the two of them? No.

The cooperating teacher was tired of dealing with the student teacher's mother.

A new cooperating teacher was found, and the formal student teaching began. Unfortunately, the student teacher became ill and did not complete the minimum number of days required to become a licensed teacher. The university took the position that it would allow the candidate to make up the time, and the new cooperating teacher said no.

The new teacher was tired of dealing with the same mother. *Mom from hell* calls the president of the university.

I couldn't make this stuff up.

There is a trend. You might think you are helping your kid. How willing are you to risk hurting them? Why aren't some of these kids telling their parents to bug out?

College is for them. Not you. Let it go.

# The Survey

I'm a science guy. I believe that data can tell a lot about what's going on with a particular problem. However, I also felt it was important to ask our students what *they* thought about the issues in this book. Would they vindicate me, or would their data of opinion blow me out of the water? The results strongly suggest that this type of student performs better in the academic setting when they are raised to "not be soft." I consulted with a college professor that specializes in data analysis and constructed a student survey that was done by a set of high school juniors in the spring of 2006. The common factors among this population are many and can generally be described in the following way.

All of the students were in a college preparatory chemistry program that is an elective course and therefore not required for graduation. The program is generally considered rigorous in nature, and that allows a wide spectrum of final grades to be given. The survey was done on a voluntary basis and involved forty-four anonymous respondents. The population was then broken down into two different groups for analysis: The first population was made up of students that had an overall grade point average of 3.0 or higher (on a 4.0 point scale). The second group had a grade point average less than 3.0. That's the only difference.

The assumption here is that the more academically successful group (GPA > 3.0) will respond in a fashion that indicates more academic constitution and less "softness" than the lower performing group. Even though it was a simple and short survey, I think you'll agree that the results support that assumption. I'm going to refer to the two groups in the results as:

Higher Performers (GPA > 3.0) and
Lower Performers (GPA < 3.0)

The actual survey is printed on the following pages, along with the average response for each group, so you can see the whole show. Many questions show nearly identical responses between the two populations, and some show huge differences. Notice that all answers were done on a sliding scale of one to five, with one being "strongly disagree" and five being "strongly agree." Will your conclusions match mine?

Please note the *average responses* of each question are printed immediately after the question.

## The Survey

This survey is designed for high school students to see how they view the way they have been raised by their parents. The survey will be done anonymously, and the group results will be used to aid the writing of a future book about high school students and their parents' attempts to raise them to be successful adults.

Some pertinent information first: Please *check* the category that best fits the household in which you were raised.

_____ My situation was the typical two-parent household.

_____ My situation was a single-parent household most of the time.

_____ My situation was being raised by neither parent but by another relative or legal guardian.

My current age is _____

My current high school grade point average (GPA) is

_____

Rate the following statements from 1–5 using the following scale:

1–Strongly Disagree, 2–Disagree, 3–Neutral/don't know, 4–Agree, 5–Strongly Agree

All questions are intended to be answered with both parents in mind as a single unit. If you were raised in a single-parent household or by a legal guardian, the questions apply to whoever raised you. The term *parents* refers to your particular situation as described above.

Please use the separate scan sheet to record your responses. Use a #2 pencil to record your responses.

Higher Performing Group=28 kids
Lower Performing Group=16 kids

Note—these are the Average Responses From Each Group (ARFEG)

1.  In general, my parents raised me effectively.

    Higher Performers=4.2

    Lower performers=4.1

2.  In general, my parents had high expectations of me academically.

    Higher Performers=4.3

    Lower performers=4.3

Your Kid's Too Soft

3. In general, my parents had high expectations for my social behavior.

> Higher Performers=4.0
>
> Lower performers=4.1

4. I go to every class every day.

> Higher Performers=4.3
>
> Lower performers=3.4

5. I am never tardy for class.

> Higher Performers=3.4
>
> Lower performers=2.8

6. I am performing academically at my highest possible effort level.

> Higher Performers=3.9
>
> Lower performers=2.6

7. I give my best effort in my classes every day.

> Higher Performers=3.8
>
> Lower performers=2.9

8. I will ask my parent(s) to excuse late absences if I oversleep.

   Higher Performers=2.7

   Lower performers=3.2

9. I have the ability to change my parents' minds when disciplining me.

   Higher Performers=2.8

   Lower performers=2.9

10. My parents never ask me if I've done my homework.

    Higher Performers=2.4

    Lower performers=2.1

11. My parents ask me if my homework is done every day.

    Higher Performers=2.9

    Lower performers=2.9

12. My parents were overly restrictive in raising me.

    Higher Performers=2.7

    Lower performers=2.6

13. I can take care of my own problems when they arise at school.

    Higher Performers=4.1

    Lower performers=4.3

14. I can take care of my own issues when they arise socially (outside of school).

    Higher Performers=4.1

    Lower performers=4.6

15. I wish my parents were more restrictive in raising me.

    Higher Performers=2.0

    Lower performers=1.9

16. My parents expect me to pay for my own material things.

    Higher Performers=3.5

    Lower performers=3.7

17. My parents do not want me to work a part-time job during the school year.

    Higher Performers=2.1

    Lower performers=2.0

18. I see my teacher for extra help when I'm confused in any of my classes.

   Higher Performers=3.9

   Lower performers=3.3

19. I believe I will be well prepared for life after high school when I graduate.

   Higher Performers=3.8

   Lower performers=3.7

20. I have taken and will continue to take challenging classes during high school.

   Higher Performers=4.4

   Lower performers=3.4

21. My parents pay me money to get good grades.

   Higher Performers=2.1

   Lower performers=1.8

22. My parents want to make my life comfortable and easy.

   Higher Performers=3.1

   Lower performers=3.1

23. My parents tell me that they had it tougher growing up than I do today.

> Higher Performers=3.6
>
> Lower performers=3.6

24. I will provide more discipline for my own kids than my parents did.

> Higher Performers=2.7
>
> Lower performers=2.9

25. My parents provide a positive and disciplined environment for me.

> Higher Performers=3.7
>
> Lower performers=3.6

26. I have acquired solid skills in high school.

> Higher Performers=4.1
>
> Lower performers=4.0

27. I am a very skilled worker at a computer, including basic typing skills.

> Higher Performers=3.9
>
> Lower performers=4.1

28. My parents will cover for me in more ways than just excusing absences.

> Higher Performers=3.0
>
> Lower performers=2.8

## The Results

There are a lot of similarities between the two groups. They both feel that they were generally raised in an effective manner, and there is a lot of positive energy for how the parents came through. I think it's pretty stunning how similarly they view questions one, two, three, twenty-two, and twenty-three. Remember, these are students that have grown up in a middle-class, suburban environment, and in homes where the parents generally care about their kid. So what are the differences that eventually guide the student performance into either the higher or lower performing group? I've boxed seven responses that the students indicate make a real difference.

### Question Four: "I Go to Class Every Day."

> High Performers=4.3
> Low Performers=3.4

I'm going to address this exact issue in chapter nine when I talk about the Four Keys to Success. The first one is "be here." No matter what you are doing, you can't be successful if you're not there. I'm not sure why our educational system struggles in this regard, but for some parents and kids, this can be a big-time challenge. Why do high school kids ditch classes anyway?

It's true that our system could re-develop a system of "lockdown," where the students are totally restricted in all movements within the school. Campuses could be totally closed for lunch, hall passes required for any movement in the building, and so on. In fact, that's how my junior high was run in 1966 when I was in the eighth grade. There is a minor segment of the parental population that wants that total control over their kid. (If you doubt that, look at the new GPS tracking systems you can employ to track your kid's location through his/her cell phone.)

The problem with total control and restriction centers on life *after* high school. At eighteen years of age, the student is either going to college or perhaps move out of the household they've been raised under. Will they be ready to function *on their own*? Will they have been prepared to make sensible choices?

The results of question four say a tremendous amount. Higher performers take fewer class periods "off" on a daily basis.

### Question Five: "I Am Never Tardy for Class."

High Performers=3.4
Low Performers=2.8

High performers land on the side of "agreement," while low performers slightly lean toward disagreement. There is, I think, a pretty obvious connection to question four here. When you get to class (or work or any other important event) on time, good things can happen at the opening bell. I try to never be late, but occasionally I have taken a hit.

In the summer of 1995, my basketball coaching staff took twenty-five players to Kansas State University for a four-day team camp. The head coach at that time was Tom Asbury, who interestingly enough, was Pomona High School's first basketball coach when the school was opened in 1973. I was a student teacher volunteer in Coach Asbury's program in 1974. Coach Asbury had become extremely successful as a college coach and had recently come to Kansas State from Pepperdine University, where he had been named the league's Coach of the Year.

Well, we drove three vans from Denver to Manhattan, Kansas, in an eight-hour caravan and left our high school parking lot at 3:30 a.m. When we arrived, we had to check in our players to the dorm, and the dorm people were not ready for us. I arrived at the first coaches' meeting at 1:07 p.m. and you guessed it, seven minutes late. As I tried to sneak in the back door, Coach Asbury saw me, stopped the meeting, and said, "I would have thought the Pomona High School coach could have at least been on time." I got ripped, and even though we had not caused the problem, Coach was right. We should have left at 3:00 a.m. One of his favorite sayings always was, "Be on time when time's involved!"

Check out the next two survey responses. They are a bit repetitive but not identical. I wanted to make sure question seven confirmed question six.

## Question Six: "I Am Performing Academically at My Highest Effort Level."

High Performers=3.9
Low Performers=2.6

## Question Seven: "I Give My Best Effort in My Classes Every Day."

High Performers=3.8
Low Performers=2.9

In many ways, these questions are the heart of the matter. How do you get your kid to produce the best possible effort on a daily or even hourly basis? The difference in response between the two groups here is gigantic. High performers are almost a four in their responses, while the low performers fall into the mid-two-plus range. I think this is the area where parents have the *greatest opportunity* to change their kids' attitudes about school.

## Question Eight: "I Will Ask My Parent(s) to Excuse Late Absences If I Oversleep."

High Performers=2.7
Low Performers=3.2

I hate to make this seem like a black and white answer, but in a way it is. Softness seems to have crept into the low performer group more than their higher performing peers. As a parent, you want to reach a point where your kid doesn't even think about asking you to do this. You can use a variety of training regimens, but you only win this battle if you refuse to cover your son or daughter in this regard. Will there be a consequence for their tardiness? Hopefully! Let the kid have the consequence.

## Question Eighteen: "I See My Teacher for Extra Help Whenever I'm Confused in Any of My Classes."

High Performers=3.9
Low Performers=3.3

It's important to remember that both groups of kids are working in our elective science program here. Among the general population of the school, they're generally *all* considered to be successful high school students. The top student group definitely shows a greater willingness to seek out help when they're confused. How important is this quality? I'm not sure I could emphasize the importance enough. My personal teaching phrase on day one with my new students is, "If you walk through that door on your free time, I'll help you until the cows come home. If you don't, I won't chase you down. You have to learn to take care of your own problems."

This is a trait that we need to all help our kids develop for the later educational times that are coming. How many of us parents recall the college professor(s) or bosses that didn't seem to care that much about us personally? Maybe attendance was never taken in our college classes. If we didn't understand something, were we willing to go get the help we needed, or were any of us intimidated? High school is the time to help your kids get through the intimidation.

Question Twenty: "I Have Taken and Will Continue to Take Challenging Classes During High School."

> High Performers=4.4
> Low Performers=3.4

National research shows a correlation between how kids perform and the willingness to take challenging courses (ACT 2005, Michigan Department of Education 2006). Different courses may or may not be considered challenging by the masses, but I think the general drift is clear. What a fine line of parenting it is to say to your child, "You will take trigonometry next year." Every parenting situation is different, but I can tell you that too many kids opt out of tougher "opportunities" today. Our school district is trying to change that direction with the introduction of curriculum that attempts to make all stakeholders aware of the need to be challenged continually.

The grade point average should not necessarily be the ultimate goal. College admission processes continually look at transcripts for "quality of coursework." Besides that, I believe that great toughness is developed only by going through tough trials. It appears that the higher performers have developed that same attitude.

I've always felt that kids' opinions should carry great weight. The answers you see in the survey are a very subtle, crying out for parenting help. They want discipline, structure, and great parenting on your part. This is the time for you, Mom or Dad, to be the provider of those services and not necessarily the time for you to be their best friend.

In summation, to be successful at anything, you must attend!

Now I want to move to the arena of how parents can build success into their kids' daily lives. There are only four things that you have to fundamentally teach them.

# Parenting 101:
# The Four Keys

I teach the concept that these "Four Keys to Success" apply to virtually *any situation in life*. We all want success, whether we're talking about education, work, family life, etc. These keys will help you and your sons and daughters get through the tough times.

## Key Number One: Be Here

How in the world can anyone succeed at anything if they don't show up to do it?

On day one of class, this gets a huge push, and I work each kid to make a commitment to the idea. I'll walk the aisles and ask them, "Can you do this? How often can you be here?" When they hesitate, I answer for them. "The answer is every day."

Hey, Mom and Dad, I know what you are thinking. "What if my little boy or little girl gets sick?" Tell them to plan on not getting sick. See, when you think that, you transfer that prepared excuse to your child. *Help them stiffen, not soften.*

Colorado television news channels ran a story a few years back about a young guy who was getting ready to graduate from his small-town high school. When he was much younger, finishing up kindergarten, his mother noted that he had not missed a single day of school during his first year. She then promised to buy him any car he wanted if completed his entire public school career without missing a single day. Are you kidding? You are talking thirteen straight years with no days off. You know how this turns out. The news stations were interviewing him two weeks from graduation, and he actually had a pretty nasty cold. He made it through, as he had countless times before, and then informed his mother he wanted a $75,000 Dodge Viper for his graduation present. Ouch!

Now, I'm not telling you to follow the above lead. Actually, I think monetary rewards for grades, cars, etc., are somewhat hollow in what they teach our young offspring. You know what I mean. Sometimes you have to do the right thing just because it's the right thing to do. Now do you remember that I mentioned earlier how Benny G. had burned me for a free steak dinner? It's not the only time that kind of thing has happened. I suppose the power of the dollar has its place in the motivational tool closet. More about that later.

## Key Number Two: Be Here on Time

Hey parents, how does the boss see it when an employee is *perennially* late to work? You know the type of worker I'm talking about. The average response is to no longer be working there. Yeah, there are exceptions to this rule, but even high school kids realize the consequences when it is a regular problem.

Our typical high school day begins with first hour at 7:25 a.m. and ends at 2:40 p.m. (the end of seventh hour). Students are generally timely to classes with two major exceptions: first hour is a major problem, and sixth hour (coming back from an off-campus lunch) is the other one. Why? You as parents may have the answer, because frankly, I just don't see it.

It must somehow relate to two of the example kids I spoke of earlier. Remember that Billy X could not solve his issue until Dad finally dealt with it. Benny G. finally developed some sense of priority through the nourishment of his stomach. The common factor here is that both of these young guys were challenged by someone who said, "It's not all right to be late." The key is that both kids changed their fatal habits. I can't even begin to count the number of high school students that have failed a class because they just couldn't get it going at an early hour.

I'm going to cover a couple of my techniques I've used over the course of thirty years of problem tardiness. These are a few of the more extreme techniques that I've used. Other examples could be given that did not work, and the student did not change their habit. Yes, it is a habit. Bad ones are hard to change.

## Sean C.—Straight-up Eighties Guy

Sean was a great kid. I mean he was intelligent, funny, and really a positive influence in class. Virtually every kid liked Sean. I remember him as a C-plus student, but what really stands out with Sean is the fact that he just could not make it to first hour "on time" twenty years ago. One day, I randomly and metaphorically went over the edge when we started class without him being there. A lesson had to be learned.

Now, I'm not sure you would agree with the technique I used, but it worked out really well, and Sean only had a few moments of mental pain to go through. Here's how it played out.

It was a beautiful spring morning in the mid-1980s as we were ready to begin class at 7:00 a.m. That's right, start times in those days were even earlier than today. Maybe we're following the educational research today that says to start the day later. Well, we're about twenty seconds into class, and I knew Sean was going to be late for the umpteenth time that semester. I had had enough and told the class to follow my lead when he arrived. Sure enough, he showed up about 7:05 with the standard apology attached. I said, "No problem, we have a lab to do today." He sat down and took out paper and pencils for his lab notes.

My class then began to follow my lead as I said, "Today's lab has a component that could be a problem but probably won't be. Statistically speaking, someone in the class may not be able to see the color change in the lab, and what's interesting is that this condition may indicate future vision issues for you as you get older." I continued with the setup by saying, "I have a special pen here that could help to identify anyone with the condition. If you can't see what's being written, let me know so we can get a heads up on the problem."

Now, you have to understand the dynamics of the setting at the time. Sean sat in the front row of the classroom, with the overhead projector right in front of him. All of the other students sat behind him, so he could not see their faces and reactions. As I began to write on the overhead, I was really careful to keep the pen just slightly above the glass, so it appeared that I was writing, but nothing was showing up on the screen. The other students were acting like it was a flock of notes, and they dutifully copied the information into their notes. It was the first time in history that every student had totally unique notes. Sean began to squint at the screen, turned his head a few times to see everyone else writing, and then back to the blank screen. Panic was beginning to set in on his face.

I finally called out the class by prompting, "I'm telling you guys that it's probable that somebody in here can't read this. Wendy—what is on the screen right now?" She quickly responded with the mythical equation, "Carbon plus oxygen yields carbon dioxide." I said, "That's right. Let's keep going." Well now, Sean was really concerned, and finally after about another thirty seconds, he blurts out, "I can't see anything!"

The class explodes in laughter, and the young victim realizes he has been had. It was a great moment in the history of PHS, but did he learn anything from it? The answer to that is "Absolutely yes." Sean never was late to first hour again, but like Benny G., Sean was close one time. The entire class thought Sean would be late on an early May morning when we heard tires squeal on the road behind the school about thirty seconds from the tardy bell. I looked out of the window and saw Sean C. throw the taxi driver a twenty-dollar bill as he sprinted to class. His car had broken down, and he wasn't ever going to be late again.

I heard an interesting discussion the other day from one of our high school administrators. Under immense pressure to raise accreditation scores, administrators start to think some crazy thoughts. This AP implied that a student shouldn't receive a poor grade because they have failed to turn work in over the course of the semester if they test adequately or above on an exam. Do you think this same guy is advocating a system where we only have two grades (midterm and final exams) for the students during the course of the semester? Not a chance. The community outcry from students and parents alike would be outrageous if daily work wasn't counted in the grading system. I'm not too worried about his comments—he just had a momentary lapse in softness himself.

---

Everyone understands the concept of extra credit in our American educational system. That is where a student has a chance to acquire some additional grading points without them counting in the overall total points. Hence, your percentage goes up. Different teachers have different philosophies on the matter, and I think a lot of different systems can work well. In fact, I routinely tell my students that I think any system can be fair as long as they (the students) understand it in the beginning. Some teachers believe in having a number of extra credit opportunities available to students. I don't.

In fact, I'm pretty lean on the concept. I've developed a position that has only one extra credit opportunity available for the entire semester. My chemistry classes are good examples of what I'm talking about. The fall semester involves an early morning opportunity that involves students coming in for one hour of extra Chemistry time at 5:00 a.m. on a designated weekday to do some extra balancing of chemical equations. The value of the extra credit was enough this past fall to raise their grades about 1.8 percent. It may not sound like much, but that's a great opportunity for the borderline kid. I had about thirty kids take me up on the chance (out of seventy-six total), and it definitely worked well for them. However, there was a catch or two.

There were some "qualifiers" to gain admittance to the extra credit session. It was designed for those that had earned an extra shot. Students had to have all of their assignments turned in for the semester in order to qualify. Up to the point of the session, that was forty-one graded assignments. If they didn't have everything in, they could come in during their free time or after school and redo the missing work in front of me. This avoids borrowing and copying someone else's old work. Secondly, if they had too many tardies (look out, periods one and six), they had to do some other atonement for admission to the session. If a student had three tardies, they had to wash desks. If they had six tardies, they had to come in and mop the floor.

Nine tardies? Mop all ten science department rooms. No one has ever completed the "nine tardy mop-fest."

Now all students understand the rules of the game in advance. Clearly, I believe in a second chance for kids, but I also believe in having consequences when they need to be in place. Let's look at spring semester Chemistry to see expectations step up in the arena of extra credit.

The second semester of Chemistry is really a tough class. It covers some deep and rigorous topics like chemical kinetics, entropy, equilibrium, acid/base chemistry, etc.

I see some parents starting to twitch out there. You remember the pain, and yet it is an incredibly dynamic course, thanks largely to my Ph.D. buddy, Tom Bindel. In the end, a large number of kids have learned to deal with a difficult body of material, developed a better work ethic, and yet they still need an opportunity to get a bit of extra credit to boost their efforts. Remember how I ran it in the fall?

Spring extra credit involves students meeting me for breakfast and doing one hour of extra work at the Denny's in the neighborhood. I came to the conclusion that it needed to be really painful and therefore issued a decree that it would start at 3:37 a.m. (this is the theoretical boundary between night and day—huh?). We work and eat breakfast until 4:37 a.m. They then leave to go home and either sleep a bit more or drink some more coffee. My students must jump through a series of qualifying hoops that are designed to see how badly they really want to do this. Here's what they look like.

1. All missing assignments must be completed as described during the fall semester.

2. All tardies must be atoned for as described above.

3. Anyone arriving late at Denny's (I mean late at all) will be sent home.

4. If you do not come to my regular class on this day (it's usually a Tuesday or Thursday), I will erase the extra credit points out of the grade book. It does not matter if your parent excuses it or not.

Does this sound harsh? *I would hope so*! One of the main goals here is to have students believe they have accomplished a very difficult task. If you can make it on time at 3:37 a.m. to do some chemistry, why can't you always make it on time to class? How has this exercise turned out in the past four years? Better than anyone envisioned.

### Year 1: Obstacles to Overcome

This whole thing started in the early spring of 2002 when a kid named Danny said to me, "Hey, Mr. S., can I do something for extra credit? I need to bring up my grade." After a short pause, I responded, "I don't do a lot of it, Danny. I think you need to just buck it up for the rest of the semester." Danny let it go for a while, but he eventually brought it back to the table a few more times. Finally, he had enlisted the whole class into the effort, and I finally relented.

"So you want some extra credit? If we do this, it has to be on my terms, and I'm telling you, it's going to get ugly." Do you like the way I fired the warning shot? One thing is really consistent about high school kids in my area—they'll do almost anything for extra credit. I then fired off the four above-described qualifications, and they didn't even blink. People started to show up to atone for the tardies and missing assignments, and yet I wasn't sure how many would actually show up on that first Tuesday insanity. So I headed for Denny's about 3:00 a.m.

What happened next was stunning: I saw kids start arriving about three fifteen, and by three thirty-five, there were fifty-four students in Denny's. *No one arrived late.* We did the acid/base work sheet for the required hour, ate huge breakfasts, and laughed a lot. I had called Denny's the day before to warn of the potential rush, and they had more waiters on call. I had a nice opportunity to talk about proper tipping, etc., and the experience was really positive. I arrived at school about 6:45 a.m. and was immediately summoned to the principal's office. Here's the context of that discussion.

> Principal D: "Hey, Smiles, I heard about Denny's, and I've got to tell you, we've got a problem."
>
> T.S.: "Morning, D. What's the problem?"
>
> P.D: "We've got parents calling. They're really upset."
>
> T.S.: "First of all, how many parents are calling?"
>
> P.D. "Two."
>
> T.S.: "Two? That's huge. I had fifty-four kids there, and two are upset? What's the issue?"
>
> P.D.: "One parent says the kids shouldn't be driving after curfew (midnight in Arvada)."

T.S.: "The only kid she needs to worry about is her own. Tell her to get herself out of bed and drive her own kid over there. No curfew violation now. What's the other issue?"

P.D.: "The other parent says this is really *unfair* to her kid."

T.S.: "Unfair? It's exactly fair. No one has baseball practice, work, a dentist appointment, etc. Everybody suffers equally. I built it based on fairness and feeling some pain. Any other issues?"

That series of exchanges illustrates how fearful the administrations of today's high schools are when a parent makes a call. How do you think the kids were in class that day, in light of the fact that they had to make it to class or suffer the "great eraser in the sky"? I remember seeing some outrageously sleepy individuals that day. Now they may have been lying across the desk, totally exhausted by 11:00 a.m., but they made it to class because they had to. No way were they going to give it up now.

I mentioned that fifty-four students qualified and came to the extra credit session in 2002. Every spring, I have four sections of Chemistry, and that total number of students is very close to 100. So in year one, around 50 percent of my students completed the exercise.

In 2003, seventy-one students completed the challenge, with the numbers similar in 2004 (seventy-six students) and 2005 (seventy-four students). I've apparently hit a fairly constant situation. How many students additionally tried to do it but arrived late at Denny's? *Exactly zero.* How many of the above students have disqualified themselves because they didn't show in our regular class? *Again, zero.*

"Today's kids will fulfill what's expected of them!"

## Key Number Three: Maximize Your Efforts

This is a pretty straightforward statement, and yet it could be hard to measure. I'm a science guy, so it's important to be able to quantify this statement with my students. How can I help today's high school kid get a grip on how hard they are busting their tails? I'll admit, it's difficult.

The only thing I've come up with in a simple way is to look at the grade book to see if everything's turned in. If an assignment comes in late, it is accepted on a very limited credit basis. I do grade checks periodically through the semester, and we always emphasize that "no blanks" is a goal we want to fulfill. That gives the kid a general guide as to how the effort card is going. But there is another tool I use to probe the kid's head.

At some point in the semester, I will ask the students to rate themselves on how their effort has been in the class. I've used different scales, sometimes worth ten points or other times worth twenty points. Then I enter the number as an assignment in the grading scheme. An interesting pattern has evolved over the years to the point that I can pretty well predict how a student is going to rate himself/herself. At times in the past, I've included "effort level" grades in the grading system. I give the students a rating on a scale of one to ten, and they do the same, with both grades being counted. Most students rate their effort *lower* than I rate it when I compare my assessment of them. This is a huge admission on their parts that they can do better. The key is to get better efforts as time goes on. I have to believe that many of our parents also find this to be a key ingredient of parenting.

## Key Number Four: Know When to Give and Get Help

This is undoubtedly the hardest key for all of humanity. It looks like the obvious application is helping kids learn more chemistry or geology when they are confused. My standard statement at the beginning of the semester is that students only have to walk through the door to receive that extra help. Most find it pretty hard to do. I think that is true for most people when asking for any form of help.

As a high school basketball coach for twelve years, I learned to deal with a lot of issues that players had that weren't about basketball. Some of those were pretty intense. The one area where we tried to deal out help for the players was in the area of academic expectations. We always tried to structure the expectation so a kid who maximized his efforts would succeed academically. That didn't mean everybody received all As and Bs in all classes. It did mean, however, that *no player* should ever go "ineligible" in our school's accountability system. I was tested on this during my first two weeks as a head coach in the fall of 1995.

I was notified that two players were academically inadequate two weeks before the start of the 1995–1996 season. One was a senior and the other a junior, and both had prospectively important roles on the team. I called them in and notified them that they were placed on academic "watch," and they had better show "significant improvement" in the next two weeks. It's a pretty complex story, but the essence is that after two weeks, neither player had met the requirement, so I had to cut them from the team.

We eventually worked out the team roles adjustments, but we had to do it without those two guys. The next time we had a player go ineligible for a week (due to failing two classes) was eight years later. Once again, kids met the expectations. If a player had to miss practice to get academic help, we would excuse them from practice.

Now I didn't have that kind of influence over my other science kids, but you know who does? *You, Mom and Dad, do.* You can suggest/require/mandate that they get the help they need to be successful. Think about it.

## Do the Four Keys Apply Everywhere?

I think the four keys apply to virtually all aspects of everyday life for everyone. Apply them to someone that is trying to make a relationship/marriage work in their life. Do they need to be there for someone else? Do they need to maximize their efforts? How about help when the relationship is on the rocks? Yes, yes, ad infinitum.

What about people that have substance abuse issues? *Again, these really apply.*

How can you, as a parent, use these? You can make them expectations in your family, just like I make them expectations in my profession. They're simple, and they are clear. You can find your own grading system for how they apply to your son or daughter.

2006, *Denny's extra credit session*

# When to Be Harsh

Wow, parenting is a really tough business. I would like to tell you that I've got it all figured out, but that's just nonsense. I do think that some things fall into general patterns of making the parental call, and therefore predictability can be an asset for a parent. Am I qualified to make the statements I am about to make? I guess the answer to that lies in looking at how my (our) own kids turned out with the Smiley System of Parenting. What do these final products look like now that they are roaming around in American society without any leashes or muzzles on them? It turned out well; I think largely because my wife, Claudia, and I were pretty much always on the same page of parenting with sons Matt (now thirty-one) and Steve (now twenty-eight).

Matt Smiley lives in the Denver area, has a job as a sales manager with a national fishing supply company, and is living his dream for ultimate jobs. He makes excellent money, travels the world representing his company, and has become a world-class fisherman. In his previous life (as a kid) he was generally easy to deal with. He was a good student and eventually graduated ninth in his class of 383. Matt went to college on a combination football/academic scholarship and graduated from college in 2001 with a degree in biochemistry. He worked in his field for three years and found it pretty distasteful. He decided to change fields, and when he interviewed for his current position in business, I asked him, "What did they ask you in the interview today? You haven't had even one business class. I'm betting you're toast."

I've thought many times about his response to that question. He looked at me and said, "It went fine. Hey, Dad, how hard can it be? I've got a degree in biochemistry. This stuff is just common sense." Now don't get me wrong. He works his butt off on a daily basis. The point is that he had prepared himself by taking a challenging pathway in the previous years. He's thirty-one, owns his own house, and makes his own decisions.

Steve Smiley is two and a half years younger and three classes behind his brother. He currently is employed at a junior college in Wyoming as the athletic director and men's head basketball coach. He has been an assistant basketball coach at three different colleges in the past, moving from jobs in Texas and South Dakota after starting his career at age twenty-three. Steve just finished his first year as the men's head coach with a record of 26–7.

He has also been an associate professor of business at

the college level during one of those stints. Steve has done a lot in his five years out of college. He finished high school as one of his class' valedictorians and went to college on a combination basketball/academic scholarship. Steve finished in five years with a degree in international business, spent the next year in Texas doing his MBA (also in international business) and graduated number one in his masters program. Even though he is only twenty-eight, Steve has published a book on his college basketball playing days as a tribute to his nationally renowned coach, Don Meyer. He married at twenty-three and is also living his dream existence.

The reason I go through this is so you can stop asking yourself that nagging question, "What does this guy know about parenting?" Most of the credit should actually go to the mother of Matt and Steve, Claudia Smiley. She never had a problem dealing out love and discipline to both of the boys. We had them *engaged* on a daily basis. *The ultimate result that matters is that the offspring can fend for themselves without anyone else controlling their lives.*

Somewhere in time you have to make some philosophical decisions on how to raise your kids. They must be conscious decisions. My personal background in this regard came from two main areas:

1. How I was personally raised by my parents, Tom and Katie.

2. The athletic background I acquired both as a player and as a high school coach.

## My Personal Upbringing

Tom and Katie Smiley were great parents but really different in how they approached the concept of raising five kids. I was number four in the pipeline, with two brothers and two sisters. Since I was the fourth kid, my parents definitely became a bit more experienced as time went on. My dad told me that they were too harsh on the firstborn brother, Carl, and they were learning how to parent in the early years. So how were they when number four, little Timmy, came along?

Mom was clearly the screamer, and Dad never even raised his voice. In fact, he was alive for my first thirty-three years on the planet, and I only heard him yell twice in those years. Mom might be caught screaming twice in five minutes. Even though they were really different, *they worked well together.* They had their system, and they had expectations for the five of us. They never *visibly* disagreed on how to deal with their offspring. In fact, it was much worse to deal with Dad's quiet disciplinary methods. The killer line I always remember was, "You know, Tim, you really disappoint me." Ouch! I would have preferred some sort of corporal punishment to that line. *But as a kid, I learned to adapt to the system that I lived under.*

It's pretty difficult to for any of us to remember multitudes of detail on the events that influenced us the most, the ones that really molded our being. One area of influence that continually shapes young peoples' lives is that of competitive athletics. It's an area that is brought in early and often to both boys and girls in American society. I probably began competitive athletics in baseball and football when I was six or seven years old. I'm sure you could find studies on both sides of the fence that say that was good and also that it was bad for a kid so young. The most important factor resides in the question of whether it was a *fundamentally positive experience* for the child. My experiences, on the whole, were very positive and very healthy in the long run. It doesn't mean there wasn't competitive heartache or disappointment along the way. On the contrary, it's the *whole spectrum* of athletic experiences that develop human character.

As a player, I worked my way through the "little leagues" of life and into high school athletics in the 1960s and 1970s. I finished my competitive "player's day" after two years of college basketball at the University of Colorado. One of the worst decisions I've ever made was to quit playing after my sophomore season in college. I did not realize that I still needed that influence in my life on a daily basis, and to this day, I wish my dad had been more willing to probe my head when I made that decision. He was used to letting his kids make their decisions at that age and then live with the consequences.

There were a lot of events that stick out as ultimate highs and lows in my playing days, and yet there are a few that I will never forget because they shaped my attitudes for a lifetime. My parents and coaches need to be thanked time and time again for helping me see life's lessons through sports.

## Nine-Year-Old Superstar (or So I Thought)

Dad was a minor league baseball player back in the day in Ohio and probably introduced me to baseball before any other sport. On a sunny Saturday morning in 1961, I was a nine-year-old pitcher in a competitive little league game. Things seemed to be going pretty well during the season, and I guess my self-esteem quotient was getting a bit too large. I was in the middle of a game, dominating the opposition the way all kids wanted to, when I received an unfavorable call from the home plate umpire. Remember that I was nine years old when I went over the edge and threw my baseball glove on the ground in disgust when the umpire called one of my pitches a ball instead of the desired strike. As the hitter was jogging down to first base, my dad leaned over into the dugout and told my coach to "take me out of the game." I don't know if the coach agreed with the decision or not, but he called me to the dugout. Without any kind of explanation, my dad said, "Let's go." He walked me to the car, and we drove home. Later in the afternoon, Papa Smiley explained the "disappointment" of seeing me throw my glove, and that's why the punishment was so swift and severe.

Think about it for just one moment. He never yelled at me. He had to be as embarrassed as a human could be on that long walk to the car. It was just a lesson I had to learn. Have you, as parents, ever had a similar opportunity to influence your son or daughter? *Did you do it?* The end result was that I never threw another glove, golf club, or any type of equipment when I was a player. Keeping it under control was the expectation.

## Senior Year—High School Football

It's fair to say that we all have many influential people in our lives. I certainly hope we have more rather than few. My life had many, and yet I would say the second most influential male on my life development probably was my high school football coach, Fred Tesone. He is still a legend of high school coaching in Colorado and developed and directed one of the best big-time programs in the state's history. I was a player for him in the earliest days of excellence and in fact, my senior year was the first time (of many) that the school's football program was ranked number one in the top classification for Colorado schoolboy football. Coach Tesone gave me my introduction to demanding more of an individual than he/she knows they can give. I like to say he "got me out of my comfort zone."

Our first game was on the typical early September Friday night in 1969, and it was a blowout win for us. Saturday morning was the beginning of the weekly cycle that was ingrained into our football dominated lives. One hour of light running and stretching, followed by about one hour of film review from the night before. Moods were light going into the film room at 10:00 a.m., and about seventy players found a folding chair in front of the screen. The film began, and like everywhere else on the athletic planet, coaches would run certain plays back and forth to make a particular point on how things could be done better. Certainly not much of that needed to be done, with the 35–0 win in the column from the night before. My eyes were about to be opened.

Sometime late in the first half, a play occurred where I

made a mistake on the film. I was a defensive end, one of the few starters back from last year's team, and probably one of our better players. On the play, I read a block wrong, got sealed to the inside, and the running back gained about five or six yards around my end. Coach Tesone called to the assistant to run that play back and then responded with, "I don't believe what I just saw." Everybody was looking at the screen as the replay went, and then I heard him say, "Mr. Smiley, do you see what I see?" The room went dead silent, and nobody looked my direction. All eyes stayed fixed on the screen. Coach T. wasn't yelling, he wasn't raising his voice, but he was questioning, and in a very subtle way, challenging me. "I don't believe your read." He ran the film back and forth *nine times* total, and it seemed like it took an hour to do it. I think the last five were done in total slow motion, and I had never felt so small in my life. My buddies told me later in the locker room how bad they felt for me when it was going on.

So how does one react to that experience? I walked out of the film room and said to myself, "I'll never let that happen again." I didn't know it at the time, but Coach Tesone had me right where he wanted me.

It's been over thirty years since I had that personal low. The season worked out pretty well (we were undefeated until the playoffs), and I finished my career as a first team all-state player for the top classification in Colorado football. There is absolutely no chance that would have happened if Coach Tesone had not challenged me the way he did in that first film session. *I was taken out of my comfort zone and had to raise my expectation levels.* I wouldn't say it was fun, but it made me stronger in a lot of ways.

---

It's probably not a good idea to just hang with the stories of "back in the day." One of the great advantages of being a high school teacher is that you stay totally current in the ways of *today's* youth. I want us to understand that these kinds of problems and solutions are with us today and just need to have the methodologies stepped up a bit. Here are some examples of parenting from both famous and average parents in our society. The common theme is that the parent(s) were able to identify a need their kid had and then apply an expectation that took their kid(s) out of their comfort zones.

### Having a Famous Father

This first parenting example is taken from an article in *ESPN the Magazine* in 2004. An article by Tom Friend called "Worlds Apart" appeared and is the story of NFL football player Tebucky Jones dealing some real world harshness on his three kids during the spring of 2004. Tebucky had reached the pinnacle of athletic success (at one time he was designated the New England Patriots franchise player) and had reaped the financial rewards that come at that level. As a brief example, Tebucky had received two different free agent signing bonuses that totaled nearly $9 million. They had a massive mansion, Xboxes and PlayStations galore, and dressed in an upscale style that included sweater vests, etc. The three kids were spoiled to the point that Dad realized that they didn't know their roots and the kind of effort he had to make to just survive on the streets during his own childhood. Maybe most importantly, the three kids, in the words of youngest son, Malique, "were getting a little bit soft." Dad made the conscious choice to change his children.

Tebucky Jones reached a point where he decided the three kids needed to see life from his point of view, and so he drove them to the neighborhood where grew up. After pulling up in his Mercedes to the Boys and Girls Club of New Britain, Connecticut, Tebucky opened the door and dropped them off in the middle of the tough zone he had lived in as a child. He told them he would be back in three hours, and the one thing they had better do was "have each other's backs. Someone messes with you, you three better mess with him." Now that's a different approach for young kids used to the privileged life. Dad felt they needed some harsh parenting.

At the end of the day, Tebucky picked up his kids and found that they had stood out like three sore thumbs and had spent their day by explaining the financial side of the family to the kids that had little or no money. Dad wanted to know if they had covered for each other, and he found out that they had indeed done exactly that. The experiment was going to continue on a weekly basis.

As the weeks rolled by, Jones's kids began to dress differently, less preppy perhaps, and began to feel more comfortable as they earned their way in the tough environment. They became more involved in the sports that were played at the club, and the young Tebucky became less shy and more aggressive on the basketball court. In essence, they came out of the protected cocoons they had lived in during their early years. The oldest daughter, Letesha, became involved in her school volleyball and softball teams when she had not shown any interest in school sports before. They all became more self-sufficient, self-confident, and "tougher."

The Jones family all benefited from shedding the softness.

## Closer to Home Harshness: Parents of High School Drivers Will Relate

In the world of parenting, no two kids turn out exactly alike. No two kids have the same experience in the so-called lessons of life. I would say that in the case of my own sons, Steve had the more traditional experience, and Matt received the more radical approach. *Different ages and different experiences dictate different methods. There is never just one answer.*

Steve Smiley was a new sixteen-year-old driver and apparently not yet very good. He had his license about for only about a month when he took the family prized 1969 Ford Bronco (mint condition with 260,000 miles on it) to Boulder, Colorado, for our high school graduation ceremony at the University of Colorado. As he left that night, he turned the Bronco around in the parking lot, and a light pole jumped out in front of him, crushing the right fender and hood. It was still drivable, and therefore, he had about a thirty-minute cushion before he encountered his parents. How would they react to the damage?

Even though it was a major problem (fifteen hundred dollars' worth) that's not uncommon to today's families; it was fixable, and it wasn't really intentional. Many times the parental reaction is something like a lecture and "don't do it again." We felt like that technique may not be a big enough deterrent to "doing it again." There had to be some kind of consequence that would make a bigger impression.

Claudia and I decided together that Steve had to have some financial pain in the repair of the vehicle. It did not matter whether we had the money to fix it or not. The decision was made to have Steve pay for half of the damage he caused. The point of this is not that he should have paid for all of it or not. You, the parent, may decide that's the way to go. That works for me. We felt a $750 payback was sufficient for his first offense. At the time, Steve said, "How am I going to pay for it?" My response was simple, "Hey, bud, get a job." Now that actually worked out really well because summer was coming, and in our family philosophy, summer jobs worked well. We did not allow either son to work during the school year because we wanted them to concentrate on their academics and the sports they were playing. Anyway, Steve got a retail job at a local warehouse and made the money to pay us back.

As I began to wrap this book up, I asked each son to write a piece for the book, and you'll find Steve's at the back of this book. One of his topics is about the "light pole" incident. I didn't realize how much he hated that summer job.

### Matt's Only Eighteen Months Old!

Young Matthew Thomas Smiley got his first dose of harshness in a less traditional way than his brother did. Matt was only about eighteen months old when he began to awaken in the middle of the night and crawl out of bed to "visit" his sleeping parents. I guess it was cute for the first couple of nights, but then it became less cute as the experience became repetitive. It happened five straight nights, and I went over the edge. I was determined to change his behavior, and that meant breaking his pattern. My method had to be effective, end the problem, and not injure Matt in any way. The technique I chose was effective, ended the problem in one night, and *did not harm him in any long-term way*. It did, however, have a controversial side that prohibited my mother from speaking to me for about a week. It seemed that we disagreed on parenting.

The local hardware store was the supply location for the spinning plastic doorknob that I bought for Matt's room. The idea was to snap this false knob over the real one on the inside of his door so that he could not grip the real knob in the middle of the night. Neither Mom nor Dad slept that night, and sure enough, we heard little feet climb out of his bed about 2:00 a.m. When the knob started spinning, I knew Matt had taken the bait. He was a bright little fellow and soon realized that he was toast. He then started to cry, pound and kick the door. He was *really* mad. This went on until five o'clock. The next three hours were filled with Claudia saying she was going to go get him. It was one of the few times we disagreed on how to handle the issue, and I was pretty adamant to *not* go get him. We held each other tightly, and it was a miserable night for all three of us.

I went to Matt's silent room a few minutes after five and had to push open the door from the outside. His little body was in a heap, sleeping against the door. I picked him up and placed him back in his bed, where he slept until about nine. We wondered what the next night would bring.

As it turned out, it brought nothing. Matt never again woke in the middle of the night and came to our room. Was it effective? Did he turn out fine? Yes, on both counts. My mother was upset enough with me that she wouldn't talk to me for about a week when she heard the story. I do acknowledge that this is a really simple example for a really simple problem. The most important point here is that it's all right to make a parental stand to solve the problem. In fact, it's the way to go. *Sometimes bigger problems indicate the need for taking bigger stands.*

# We're All Responsible

I love the two terms *old school* and *new school*. They can mean so many things and be used in so many areas. As they apply to parenting, it can't be said that either way is always the way to go. Many parents would point to some example of "old school coaching" that they had experienced many years ago and are now remembered in a positive light. Doesn't the old school method always work?

Old school methods of coaching high school football used to include a very dangerous practice. Coaches would not allow water on the field during practice, no matter how hot it was. They thought this practice promoted mental toughness, and I guess maybe it did. *The problem was, it was an extremely dangerous way to promote it.* Today we know that every athlete must be properly hydrated, and therefore, coaches had to find other ways to build the young mind. *You, the parent, must raise your kid to be mentally tough without going into extremely dangerous zones.*

Hey, Mom and Dad, this is chapter eleven. You're still with me. You must believe raising quality young people (the kind that can stand on their own and positively impact our society) is an important thing for all of us to do. It is going to take contributions from many angles in society, *including* parents, teachers, administrators, etc. Every facet has a responsibility, and this book has mostly addressed the parental end of it. So how's the educational system working in doing its part? I think the report card is a mixed bag.

## School System Softness

I recently finished a meeting with our high school administration, and I'm beginning to realize that they've lost some focus on what's good for kids. They seek short-term gains without thinking about the long-term impact of some of their decisions. *This is a really dangerous mistake.*

Two recent meetings with my administration discussed some disturbing data, and I have struggled with their problem-solving approaches. Our graduation rate has recently dropped, and justifiably, there's a major concern being expressed. In fact, I think it is one of the scariest indicators to ever come to our school. In one year, the rate dropped from 93 percent to 84 percent. I can't ever remember seeing it out of the nineties in my entire thirty-two years at Pomona. So why has it dropped? *I mean, that is the next question to ask, isn't it?*

Shockingly, our administrative leadership hasn't even

asked the question. They thought the only important thing was to stop the slide and improve the numbers. Principal Guy (not his real name) says that teachers must do more to remediate the kids that are failing and therefore raise the number of kids passing. To be fair, he never said teachers should "soften" the curriculum or change our standards for the students. *But once again, have we looked at why they are failing at this historically high rate?*

One of the teachers in this meeting noted that the failing students may have had a number of home environment issues that were out of the realm of a teacher's control. Principal G. responded with a statement to the effect that he can't control bad parenting, so we had to solve the issue in our *classroom approach*. Discussions were held about remediation, retaking of exams, etc. We (teachers) have to help them get through high school and therefore raise that graduation rate back to an acceptable standard. I was, and continue to be, of a different mindset. I have known for a long time that if the kids have developed solid work ethics and habits, the testing situation will take care of itself. I want *a long-term approach*.

I left that meeting in a bit of a confused state and in general, really bothered. "Something is missing here," I told myself. "Something's just not right." Two hours of my personal planning time was all I needed to discover the root of the problem. With an investment of three additional hours (now a total of five man hours) I believe I have found the problem, backed it up with quantifiable data and research, and presented a viable solution. I'm a long way from being a genius, but the problem was not that complex. Here's how the problem-solving session went.

My science department colleagues had informed me at the previous lunch that there were only two categories of failures in their classes. One group consists of kids that "just can't do it" and the other category harbors a group that just "*won't* do it." Now remember that I have tremendous respect for this group of teachers. Countless numbers of former students have returned to thank these people for their positive influences that were bestowed on them when they attended Pomona.

Three Ph.D.s have taught in our department, but I know that you are not yet convinced. Like Principal Guy, you want data as proof of the strength. Here's a chunk. In 1999, there were eleven valedictorians on the stage at graduation. I'll repeat those numbers: eleven outstanding young women and men. With all of their futures wide open, ten of the eleven had decided to major in the sciences (or engineering) with a lone wolf predicting that business would be his major. Ten of eleven! This certainly represents a strong department.

Anyway, to be a bit repetitive, the science department informed me at the above-mentioned meeting that there are only two categories of failures: those students that *can't do it* and those students that *won't do it*. So I asked what percentages of all failures reside in each class, and my compatriots stunned me with the following: *5 percent can't and 95 percent won't. It dawned on me that we better address the 95 percent in a hurry.*

The following morning found me looking for three

examples of kids that have chosen to not follow the guide-lines of classical student achievement in our school system. John was a first hour junior student in one of our chemistry sections. This kid had fourteen unexcused tardies and absences in the first ten weeks of the semester. I think that's outrageous (remember the four keys to success). Various methods of discipline had been attempted by the teacher, and the kid was unresponsive. Yes, the parents were contacted, and the discussions did not change J.L's behavior.

Example two was found in a freshman Earth Science student, and she had a similar story to tell. Fifteen unexcused tardies and absences marked her record.

The third kid is the crown jewel of how "not to be a student." Billy (not his real name) had eighty-four total unexcused tardies and absences in his classes for the first ten weeks. I didn't stutter. Eighty-four. I then personally contacted all three of these students within the hour and asked them two questions. The first one went like this. "Has any administrator contacted you about your attendance?" All three said the same thing, "No."

The second question was really the heart of the matter. I then asked each of them, "If an administrator came to you with some type of consequence, like mopping floors or coming in for Saturday school (recall the movie, *The Breakfast Club)* how would you respond?" Again it was unanimous. "I would change what I'm doing."

I'm embarrassed to admit what I found out the next day. In conducting a search through the school's database, I found 151 PHS students that had accrued ten or more unexcused absences during the first twelve weeks of school. The disease had clearly grown beyond just a few kids. Why? Because of a lack of consequences!

I continued my data search and found another stunner. A total of 383 students (almost one quarter of our entire population) had missed forty or more class periods (roughly equal to seven total days) in the first sixty days of school. *Again, there was no administrative move to address these students' actions.* Could this be the reason for our declining graduation numbers? It's more than a "maybe." My final act of data gathering occurred the next day when I informally surveyed my juniors and seniors in my Chemistry classes (about eighty total kids). With a show of hands, I asked them to share their opinions with me regarding their view of the administration's stance on timeliness in the school. "Please raise your hand," they were told, "when you wish to vote in one of three categories."

1. You feel the administration is too strong in the area of attendance enforcement.

2. You feel the administration is too soft in the area of attendance enforcement.

3. You are neutral when considering number one and number two above.

Guess the results of how the students saw the issue in my classes. One student voted in category one above. Thirty-seven voted in category number two.

## More Data on the Problem

The spring of 2008 gave our science department another opportunity to analyze the success ratios of our students. We now have two years of sub-90 percent graduation rates (84 percent and 87 percent for the two most recent years of data). Our department once again went on the analysis train and looked at our Science Department failures for the first half of the spring 2008 semester. What we found is that the student failures had again occurred mostly due to attendance issues.

We looked at 228 students that were failing after forty days of class time. This occurred in forty-nine total classes with twelve different teachers. On average, 62 percent of the failing students (142 total) had missed at least five days of classes. That's a minimum of 12.5 percent absenteeism. Can you, Mom or Dad, be gone 12.5 percent of the time from your job? Many of these students had missed *ten days or more*.

Our department cares a lot about the success of the students at Pomona. At the time of this writing, we are encouraging (battling?) our administration to get a grip on these kids and their attendance problems. Check out Appendix A for the summation of this data. Our current system has allowed kids to fall through the attendance crack. For over twenty years, our high school had an assistant principal that did nothing but chase wayward kids on attendance issues. The new system has not dedicated a position to the cause, and instead, *shares* the responsibility with four assistant principals.

You know what that means? *Nobody is doing the job*! How does a student have eighty-four or more infractions and not get contacted? How can 151 students have ten or more unexcused absences? I'm not saying people aren't busy, nor am I saying they don't work hard. They do. But all of our administrators' energy had been directed to chase the tail of the raising the standardized test score. *The source of the problem had not been addressed.*

Assistant principals have been directed to spend time in classrooms and then analyze the quality of the teacher's presentation. *Does the teacher have his/her learning goal of the day on the board?* The priority does not match the problem. Kids have always needed guidance in developing their social habits. *Our educational system has gone soft, just like the parenting I've been talking about for eleven chapters now.* So where does the solution lie to the graduation rate problem? As it turns out, it lies in the great northwest.

---

The state of Washington passed a law in 1995 that directly addressed this issue. The law forced school districts to address truancy (unexcused absences) from the first one on. Parents had to be contacted immediately, and the consequences increased if the offense continued. Here's the simple summary of what happened:

The enrollment rate for kids in school had been dropping for a number of years in Washington. As soon as the policy went into effect, the rate began to rise, and so did the graduation rates. All of the math is there for you math geeks, but the main point is clear:

"Address the problem, and you will probably solve it!"

Now will we solve our issue at Pomona? I really am not sure. Principal Guy called me in to tell me he had read through my brochure and found the data interesting or amazing or whatever. I really wasn't paying much attention to it. What I did want to know was whether he was going to change his administrative structure to solve the problem. He was kind enough to ask for my opinion on who should head up the solution by becoming the next "attendance czar." It really doesn't matter, as long as someone does it, and does the job thoroughly. So the essence is, we shall see whether or not the system steps up with the firmer approach that students and the school need.

# Lines in the Sand

Do you ever draw that proverbial "line in the sand?" I'm not sure that there is a more difficult question for a parent than this one. You can't be drawing lines in the sand all the time, or none of them will be clear. Allow me to illustrate with a quick story from my first few years of teaching.

Two instances stick out from the early days, and I would say they both illustrate how "not to teach effectively." The first one involves a student teacher in our science department in the late seventies, during a time when we operated on a year-round schedule. The school operated twelve months a year with only a few common days off around the holidays. As a result, teachers and students were constantly coming and going. The typical shift would involve being in school for four months and then having a two-month vacation. Three "tracks" were involved with the ingenious names Track A, Track B, and Track C.

It was early April, and I was coming in for my first day of the new shift. All of the school's teachers were in attendance for a couple of "overlap" days, so it was a great chance to catch up on the past two months. As I walked through the glass doors of the science area, there was a horrific sound coming out of room 7A immediately to my left. A totally unfamiliar adult voice was screaming at the students to the point that I poked my head in the doorway to make sure everything was all right. It's hard to describe what my eyes saw.

An unknown young adult female was teaching the class and was extremely upset with the students. She was screaming at them, and I guess I would say "demanding" their attention. Well, she wasn't getting it, and in fact, the kids were acting if she wasn't even in the room. *The more she screamed, the louder they got.*

I wandered into the science office thoroughly confused and found one of our teachers sitting at his desk. When I inquired what was going on, he buried his head in his hands. It seems that I had encountered his "student teacher," and she was in her final days there at PHS. While our staff member had worked hard to help the student teacher adapt, it just wasn't meant to be. She did not pass her student teaching experience, and it mercifully ended a few days later.

How many lines in the sand do you think were drawn for the kids in that class? Calculators may be needed to find that answer. Does this experience resemble any of our own experiences raising our kids? It may or may not involve voices that get really loud. Do we draw lines in the sand every day? Maybe we rarely have to do it. Every possibility exists in between those two extremes.

The second example of how not to teach comes from a Pomona teacher in another department in the early 1980s. There's no need to involve names here, but suffice it to say the kids called her "The Screaming Flea." S.F. operated in another world, one in which she would have control of her students, no matter what. I remember kids would come in to my class in disbelief following an hour in her class. She had a list of "rules" or "lines in the sand" that were truly amazing. It took two class periods at the beginning of each nine-week quarter to cover her rules. One of them went like this. "If you are standing here when the bell rings, you are tardy." She then took two steps deeper into her room and I guess crossed some imaginary line. "If you're here, you are not tardy."

I've operated for thirty-three years with one basic unwritten rule for classroom behavior. "Always deal with people in my room from a basis of respect." I never felt the need for anymore rules. Do I deal with kids on the rare occasions that they break this single mantra? Yes, every time. The point is then made and kids know where the line is. The funny thing about this is that I had to recently ask a couple of young bulls to leave my first hour class. They were flopping around and struggling, being disrespectful as someone else was explaining some chemistry. I thought about how long it had been since the last time I had to ask a student to leave. I guess it had been a couple of years. It doesn't have to happen very often to be effective.

## Everyday Parenting and Lines in the Sand

What are the *critical issues* of the day in 2010 parenting? I'm talking about the ones where you have to have the unbending stance. Let's take this chronologically, starting with young kids. You see, it goes from simple to complex. How often have you said to yourself, "Life's issues were a lot simpler when the kids were younger?" Do you remember the early days of parenting when you concocted a list of things that the kid absolutely couldn't do? For the most part, the items on this list were based on their personal safety. I think it's interesting that this list has largely stood the test of time. Most parents have a variation of this list. Here are *some* of the items that made it onto Claudia and Tim Smiley's list in the 1980s. Notice how the order goes from toddler to college kid.

- You can't go in the street. It's too dangerous.
- If you can't swim, you can't go in the deep end of the pool.
- You have a curfew, be in by _____.
- Call if you are going to be late.
- Are you getting sleepy when driving? Pull over and sleep.
- Go to class and turn your stuff in.
- No drinking and driving.

If you don't have a list or a starting point, use ours, and then add your own items. The key here is that the items on the list are absolutely necessary in your view. But remember to keep it simple. You don't need the screaming flea in your system.

# A Final Word

In the final analysis, I wanted to write the book because I felt I recognized a problem, and I could offer a solution that would work. As a parent, your job in the year 2010 is more difficult than mine was in the 1980s. But that's the progression. The world *is* more complex, *but it's important to realize that you can solve your problem.* The solution is easier than you think, and the main component of it is the parent has to step up and deal with their child. It doesn't need to be nasty or bitter. *Just deal with it.*

That kid that pissed me off in April 2004 with his tardiness deserves a big thank you in early 2010. In the middle of my four-year quest, I caught an interview on Denver's Channel 2 News on the morning of August 21, 2006. Lou Holtz of ESPN fame (and a mega-successful college football coach) answered a question with a comparison to parenting. At the time, I thought, "That pretty well sums up my book."

The remark was about having to confront a difficult issue or decision in life. In Lou's words, "It's a little bit like being a parent. You can't worry whether your children like you or not." That's exactly the mistake herds of parents have made. *You can't always be your child's best friend.*

I have to take a moment and talk about the educational system's responsibility in the whole scheme of making resilient children. I currently see a dangerous approach to cultivating "success" in today's high school environment. It is called "credit recovery." Recent administrators that I have seen are proponents of helping students "recover" lost credits in some very illegitimate ways. They like a concept they call Week Thirty-seven (thirty-six weeks in the normal school year), where they want teachers to offer some extra catch-up work for an extra week that is then used to help failing students acquire their lost credit. This only encourages students to not honor deadlines and timeliness. Last time I checked, those two things still exist in the work world.

The notion gets really absurd when the system provides an online make-up course that replaces the regular class that was previously failed. Hey, explain this to me. How do you replace a lab intensive science class like Biology or Chemistry by sitting at a computer terminal for a few extra hours? People that tell you this is legitimate education are delusional. This system does, however, help school administrators portray their graduation rates in a more favorable light. Remember, I want to make our kids tougher, not softer. As parents, you need to resist this concept if it is dealt to your child.

I have included a couple of appendixes that show my research on some of these issues. One is a blank survey to use with your child to compare to the earlier reported results. I hope you have enjoyed the book and find it useful. As I prepare to sign off from this broadcast, I include closings by both of my sons. I think one of the ultimate signs of your personal success as a human being comes in the form of your children. I am immensely proud of Matt and Steve. The difference now from when they were younger is that they are no longer under my influence of formation. They are their own men. I want you to feel that same level of success at the end of twenty-five years. You can help them to *mold themselves* into symbols of human quality and personal success. But you better hurry. You only get one shot, and the clock is running.

P.S. Is this stuff still going on in my classroom? Sure. Kids want to toughen up and can basically be cajoled into whatever. Here's the latest from room 421.

> T.S.: Hey guys. How many of you want to shovel some rock?
>
> Kid A: Why would I want to do that?
>
> T.S.: Because it's hard. You could get some blisters.
>
> (Now there's a distinctive pause in the class, maybe four or five seconds.)
>
> Kid B: I'll do it.

And the rest is history. In late May of 2008, twelve of my Chemistry students made the illogical choice to shovel 1,500 pounds of crushed granite rock out of the back of my truck and into a chalked up circle we drew on the ground in the student parking lot. We then shoveled them back into the truck, out onto the ground again, and finally back into the truck a second time. The group would tell you it was both voluntary and exhilarating.

Why? Because it was hard.

So now, in final analysis, if I can get high school kids to do something as senseless as shovel rocks without a reason, what can their parents get them to do when it really matters? Help your kid learn to value doing the difficult deed. It will always be more valuable than being soft. When the time comes to take drivers' education, make Junior drive the stick shift in the middle of a busy boulevard. And when they do, encourage them endlessly, and exercise great patience when they fail. If you do, they will succeed in the moment and in life.

I have spent thirty-four years of my life trying to do what is best for kids. I will continue to help them prepare for their lives after high school with one thing in mind. I will ask myself whether the student will be more independent and able to take care of themselves in the future as a result of my work. *No test score will ever be more important than that.*

Thanks for listening to an educational soldier.

# Afterword One

## By Steve Smiley

I think there are a lot of ways in which parents, teachers, or any authority figures can try to motivate kids to work hard, be successful in school, and eventually prepare themselves to be successful in life. I also think, however, that as the years pass, this is undoubtedly getting harder and harder to do. I'm not going to even attempt to act like I'm the authority figure on the issue of kids being too "soft" these days, being that I'm only in my mid-twenties right now and possibly haven't learned all of the lessons that others may have.

I do know this, however. I'm five months away from having my first child as I'm writing this, and I'm scared to death that my kids will be too soft because of the way society is now treating them. As you read through this book, you will see a lot of examples of how kids are becoming too soft. I would assume that my father, Tim Smiley, is as much of an authority figure on the matter as anybody else, as he has seen countless kids go through the halls of the high school he has worked at for thirty-plus years, and how he has seen those kids get softer and softer as they get babied by their parents, by administrators, and by society in general.

I took my dad's Chemistry class when I went to Pomona High School, and it was one of the classes where there were expectations. You were expected to be to class on time, you were expected to ask questions and participate, and you were expected to do your work. If you didn't, there was no sympathy when grades were posted at the end of the semester. I found it interesting that while his class was in the minority because of those expectations, time and time again he was selected as the keynote speaker to prestigious events like senior baccalaureate, senior tea, and graduation. When I look back on it now, I think he was popular because students like expectations. They like discipline, and they like direction. He provided that in his classes, and the students responded.

Today, I don't think that society in general puts enough expectations on our youth. Our children are allowed to be lazy, their parents call them in when they are late for school, and there are no repercussions. I don't think that my dad allowed that to happen when I grew up, and I can think of a certain story that will clarify what I'm talking about. I can remember when I finally turned sixteen years old, and I received my driver's license. I had prepared for six months with my driver's permit, and I felt that I was ready to hit the road as I began to gain some independence. It wasn't one week into being a licensed driver that I rammed my 1969 Ford Bronco into a light post on a rainy night. I didn't have enough vision, and I smacked into a concrete light post in the middle of a parking lot. I really didn't know what to do, so I drove the car home for the remainder of the night, and when I got home, I told Pops what had happened. He said he would take a look at things in the morning.

The next morning, as I was showering and getting ready for school, I heard the door open, and my dad was not happy, to say the least. The "minor" scrape that I had described to him the night before when he was in a half-sleep was in reality a much bigger deal. The whole front right side of the car was totaled, and it would cost a lot of money to fix it. At this point in time, he had to make a decision, and I think it is in situations like these that most parents fail. He decided that instead of saying it was okay, and he was just happy that I wasn't hurt, I would instead have to get a job to pay for the damage. It wouldn't have sunken the family for him to pick up the bill, but this was a prime opportunity to teach his son a lesson about responsibility. While I didn't mean to wreck the car one week into my driving career, that car was still wrecked and something had to happen. So he made me get a job to pay for the damages. I had to go the next day to the now-extinct Service Merchandise Company and get a job working as a cashier and warehouse boy. I absolutely despised every minute of working there, but I worked for an entire summer, forking over the money to pay for the car until the bill was paid off.

I really believe that if my dad would have paid that bill, I would have become softer. I wouldn't have learned the lesson that with more freedom and independence comes more responsibility. And that is what his message is all about. Today, when students skip class because they didn't have the discipline to get up and get to school, their parents save them. What type of lesson does that teach the kid? Is it okay to not show up for your responsibilities? And then parents wonder why their students, who scraped through high school, don't do well in college and then do even worse with the real test, making it in the "real world." There comes a point in time where the parent can no longer save the child, but when that time comes, if the parent has continued to rescue his or her child for eighteen years, it's too late.

Hopefully, this book will inspire you to take the harder road, to tell your children it's not okay when they screw up, to tell them that the words *responsibility* and *accountability* aren't curse words. I know that I learned a life full of lessons growing up in my household, and I'm grateful for the teachings of my parents and for the fact that they didn't bail me out when I messed up.

Dad, thanks for all that you have already taught and for everything that you still teach me on a daily basis,

—Your youngest,
Steve

# Afterword Two

## By Matt Smiley

There have been many times in my life when I've thought about how whacked out my dad is. When he locks on a mission, it can be overwhelming.

I know he has talked with you about how I worked into my job with my current company. It's a true story told earlier in this book about Dad questioning my interview with the new company and my subsequent response, "Hey how hard can it be? I've got a degree in biochemistry." Well it turns out, this job is *very* demanding. My experiences in college (both academic and athletic) prepared me well for the real world. It was demanding in many ways, but the important thing is that *it was worth it.*

Challenging yourself in college is an important step to preparing for life after school. It was pretty typical for many athletes to major in as easy of a field as possible. And who can blame them really? When you are dedicating thirty-plus hours a week during the season, and still twenty-plus in the off season, it is easy to take the easy way out in your class schedule. The problem with that is it doesn't do much for you when you graduate and realize you haven't really challenged yourself at all academically. Nor do you have a degree that is very well suited to being successful in the next phase of life. I have learned that it is not as important what degree you get, as long as the *process* of getting it prepares you for life after college. Though my current career has nothing to do with my biochemistry major, the rigors of obtaining such a difficult degree did more for preparing me for my current job than you can imagine. Throughout the course of studying biochemistry, I endured many long nights studying, typically after already being completely worn out from football practices and or games. I learned that you can do things that are extremely hard even when you are already near the edge of being completely exhausted. It prepares you for those tough days in the office once you get out of school. Even the *hardest* days I experience in the office these days fail in comparison to closing the library down at two a.m. preparing for that Organic Chemistry final the next day. If you challenge yourself and survive it in college, you will be that much better off once you get out of school.

Succeeding is not something that comes easy. It requires going that extra mile when you have the ability to do so, and making yourself better in the process. By working hard and setting out to challenge yourself in everything you do, you are preparing yourself for what will become some of your many successes in the future. If I were to name the most important lesson that I have learned from my dad, it would be to never shy away from the things that are hard. In fact, seek them out. You will be much better off for putting yourself through the most challenging situations when the opportunities arise. Once you have accomplished your most challenging goals, you will see that the rewards are so much greater than if you had chosen to just do it the easy way. This is without a doubt one of the most important mindsets that my dad instilled in me starting at a young age. You would be doing your child well to do the same.

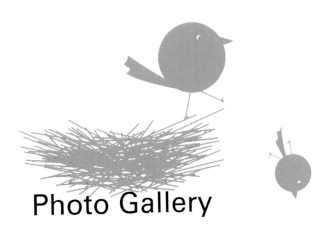

# Photo Gallery

*"The Toughest Kid," Daniel Lazzati, coun-
selor Cheryl, and daughter*

*Daniel Lazzati*

*Daniel's sweet home*

*Daniel's sweet home*

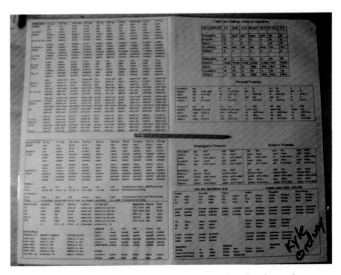

*Kyle Ordway prepares for a ten-point Latin quiz*

*Student contributing authors*
*(from left: Andrew, Hannah, Monica, and Jake)*

**Rocks 'R Us**

May 9, 2008

Hey Mr. Smiley,

     My son/daughter _____ really wants to shovel a few rocks. Could you please help them find some? Also, would it be possible to have them use an 1875 coal shovel from the glory days of the railroads? Thanks.

Parent Name _____     Parent signature_____

*Parent permission slip for shoveling rocks*

*Students pumping up with shovels*

*The Smiley family, Matt, Grandma
Dorothy, Claudia, and Tim*

*Steve, Nikki, and the legendary Madden*

# Appendix A

Student Failure and Absenteeism

# The Correlation of Student Failure and Absenteeism
# Pomona Science Department
# March 9, 2008

Science Department Data Spring 2008
Semester through March 7, 2008

Forty (40) days of the semester completed. Five (5) absences represent having missed 1 full week of school (12.5% of the total class time). This is an absenteeism rate that the Science Department finds unacceptable.

| | E.S. Teacher A | E.S. Teacher B | E.S. Teacher C | E.S. Teacher D | Bio Teacher A | Bio Teacher B |
|---|---|---|---|---|---|---|
| # of Sections | 5 | 2 | 5 | 3 | 4 | 5 |
| #F Students | 18 | 9 | 20 | 9 | 30 | 43 |
| F's w/5+ Absences | 12 | 7 | 13 | 6 | 20 | 25 |
| | | | | | | |
| % of F's w/5+ absences | 66% | 77% | 65% | 66% | 67% | 59% |
| | | | | | | |

Why was this study done?

The Science Department at Pomona High School recently received data on the large number of F's among our students in our classes. The number is larger than it should be and consequently, we seek the reasons for the inflation.

What does the data show?

*If you don't go to class, you will probably fail.*

| Bio Teacher C | Bio Teacher D | Chem Teacher A | Chem Teacher B | Chem Teacher C | Phys Teacher A | Phys Teacher B | Totals |
|---|---|---|---|---|---|---|---|
| 2 | 4 | 4 | 2 | 4 | 5 | 4 | 49 |
| 16 | 21 | 11 | 15 | 17 | 13 | 6 | 228 |
| 11 | 13 | 6 | 10 | 11 | 6 | 2 | 142 |
| | | | | | | | |
| 69% | 62% | 55% | 67% | 65% | 46% | 33% | 62% |
| | | | | | | | |

# Appendix B

## The Survey

This survey is designed for high school students to see how they view the way they have been raised by their parents. The survey will be done anonymously, and the group results will be used to aid the writing of a future book about high school students and their parents' attempts to raise them to be successful adults.

Some pertinent information first: Please *check* the category that best fits the household in which you were raised.

_____ My situation was the typical two-parent household.

_____ My situation was a single-parent household most of the time.

\_\_\_\_\_ My situation was being raised by neither parent, but by another relative or legal guardian.

My current age is \_\_\_\_\_

My current high school grade point average (GPA) is

\_\_\_\_\_

Rate the following statements from 1–5 using the following scale:

1-Strongly Disagree, 2-Disagree, 3-Neutral/don't know, 4-Agree, 5-Strongly Agree

All questions are intended to be answered with both parents in mind as a single unit. If you were raised in a single-parent household or by a legal guardian, the questions apply to whoever raised you. The term *parents* refers to your particular situation as described above.

Please use the separate scan sheet to record your responses. Use a #2 pencil to record your responses.

1. In general, my parents raised me effectively.

2. In general, my parents had high expectations of me academically.

3. In general, my parents had high expectations for my social behavior.

4. I go to every class every day.

5. I am never tardy for class.

6. I am performing academically at my highest possible effort level.

7. I give my best effort in my classes every day.

8. I will ask my parent(s) to excuse late absences if I oversleep.

9. I have the ability to change my parents' minds when disciplining me.

10. My parents never ask me if I've done my homework.

11. My parents ask me if my homework is done every day.

12. My parents were overly restrictive in raising me.

13. I can take care of my own problems when they arise at school.

14. I can take care of my own issues when they arise socially (outside of school).

15. I wish my parents were more restrictive in raising me.

16. My parents expect me to pay for my own material things.

17. My parents do not want me to work a part-time job during the school year.

18. I see my teacher for extra help when I'm confused in any of my classes.

19. I believe I will be well prepared for life after high school when I graduate.

20. I have taken and will continue to take challenging classes during high school.

21. My parents pay me money to get good grades.

22. My parents want to make my life comfortable and easy.

23. My parents tell me that they had it tougher growing up than I do today.

24. I will provide more discipline for my own kids than my parents did.

25. My parents provide a positive and disciplined environment for me.

26. I have acquired solid skills in high school.

27. I am a very skilled worker at a computer, including basic typing skills.

28. My parents will cover for me in more ways than just excusing absences.